D0462177

A New Kind
of Church

A New Kind of Church

Understanding Models of Ministry for the 21st Century

Aubrey Malphurs

BakerBooks

Grand Rapids, Michigan

© 2007 by Aubrey Malphurs

Published by Baker Books
a division of Baker Publishing Group
P.O. Box 6287, Grand Rapids, MI 49516-6287
www.bakerbooks.com

Printed in the United States of America

Library of Congress Cataloging-in-Publication Data
Malphurs, Aubrey.
    A new kind of church : understanding models of ministry for the 21st century /
Aubrey Malphurs.
        p.   cm.
    Includes bibliographical references and index.
    ISBN 10: 0-8010-9189-6 (pbk.)
    ISBN 978-0-8010-9189-6 (pbk.)
    1. Mission of the church—North America. 2. Church work. I. Title.
BV601.8.M35 2007
262.001′7—dc22   2006026116

Contents

Introduction

I took one look at Pastor Bill and knew something was seriously wrong. He had dark circles under his eyes, and they looked puffy. So I asked him how much sleep he was getting these days. He confided in me that he slept little, and it was beginning to tell on him. He also looked gaunt, and his wife was beginning to worry about him. What was his problem? Did he have some serious physical ailment, such as heart trouble or maybe even cancer? No. What was happening to him was likely worse, depending on your perspective.

Several months earlier, one of Pastor Bill's key staff persons resigned to pursue ministry elsewhere. When people asked about his resignation, the staff person confided that he didn't agree with the church's direction. The church could be called a seeker church and included elements of the Purpose-Driven Church model. The church's leadership didn't realize that some others in the church felt the same way as this staff person but had remained silent. The staff person's leaving served as the catalyst for these disgruntled people to coalesce.

As word got out about the resignation and the reason prompting it, this minority began to express itself in a number of ways. First, they talked among themselves, discussing the resignation, their empathy for the staff person, and their dissatisfaction with the church. Second, they began to show up at board meetings to verbalize their discontent. And third, several wrote letters, some very extensive and harsh, to the board as to why they believed the church was moving in the wrong direction.

Bill and his staff didn't just sit back idly and watch all this take place. They went to countless meetings, both public and private, to explain themselves and what they were seeking to accomplish. At times they felt as if they were ministry firemen, spending much of their valuable time fighting fires rather than igniting fires for Christ in their community. Their efforts helped to some extent, but just about the time they thought they had put out the fire, it would reignite, making matters even worse. What had been a dream job was turning into Bill's worst nightmare.

Most good leaders have the same fatal flaw—they like to please people and keep them happy. And when people aren't happy and complain, leaders aren't happy. This was true of Pastor Bill. Furthermore, his church had been growing, due in large part to its outreach focus on Sunday morning and its evangelism ministries. Bill and the staff had worked hard, very hard, at keeping the church focused on outreach, and the result was significant conversion growth. Now all was in jeopardy. In fact, Bill was in enough emotional pain that he was finding it increasingly difficult to resist thoughts of resignation that had recently begun to nag him.

A Familiar Story

Chances are very good that you are familiar with such a situation as Bill's. Perhaps his story is your story. In some way you can identify with this man and his church. It may be that you are a member of a church that has been through a similar experience. If not, it's likely that you know of a church somewhere close that has, and you're wondering what is going on. Or maybe you are part of a group in a church that is struggling with the church's current direction. The leaders are not doing church the way you think it should be done. And you ask, Why is all this taking place?

The twentieth century as a whole was a time when we didn't see a great deal of change, at least nothing like what we've seen toward the end of the twentieth century and into the twenty-first century. Widespread change is also being reflected in America's churches. During most of the early to middle twentieth century, there was a typical, traditional way we did church, and a large number of people attended church, especially in the South.

As we've transitioned into the twenty-first century, however, the number of churched people has decreased considerably, and several new church models have been planted on American soil. In addition, to address demands for change, some established churches have transitioned and adopted new ways of doing church. The problem is that, while they claim to be churches, they don't look like the church, at least not the traditional church model that was the norm during much of the twentieth century.

There are all kinds of labels for these new models, such as emerging churches, megachurches, seeker churches, Purpose-Driven churches, cell churches, connecting churches, contemporary churches, house churches, new-paradigm churches, postmodern churches, and so on. For example, I'm aware of one church that seeks to combine what it believes is the best of the seeker church model with the Purpose-Driven Church model.

Church names don't sound familiar either. Some I've heard are Mars Hill, Journey, Crosswalk, the Highway Community, Warehouse, Next-Wave, Solomon's Porch, Liquid Church, and Mosaic. What happened to good old First Church Downtown? I firmly believe that we "ain't seen nothin' yet." There's more, much more, to come.

New-Model Churches

Some important questions are: Are these new-model churches really churches? How can we know? Or are they some weird aberration or cult in "church clothing"? And worse, are they taking us down some slippery slope that will not only dilute the church's impact but lead it into doctrinal heresy? Should we sing their praises or throw stones?

Some people have opted for throwing stones, describing these churches and what they do in derogatory, emotional language. They might say these churches are "taking their cues from the world," "slick," or just "entertaining." However, if we can get beyond their offensive language, I believe we can learn from the critics of the new-paradigm churches as well as from the churches themselves.

The major issue we must address is wrapped up in this question: Is there a standard model for doing church? Does the Bible give us a correct, prescribed model that we're all to follow? If so, is it more like today's traditional or contemporary format? If not, then is each church free to develop its own model? Are there any biblical guidelines for this?

Why This Book?

There are several reasons why I've written this book. First, it's grown out of my love for the local church. I believe that Bill Hybels is correct when he says the church is the hope of the world. Jesus said this in Matthew 16:18. Second, my love for Christ's church has led me to study the various church models, and I would like to share what I've found. Third, my experience as a consultant with churches where some infighting is taking place has raised my concern over what critics of the new-paradigm churches are saying.

I worked with one church where the critics caused great harm to the church, its outreach, the pastoral staff, and the pastor in particular. It took a huge emotional toll. He, like Pastor Bill, didn't get much sleep at night. I took the opportunity to engage at least one of the church's detractors so that I could learn more about such critics and how they think. Some of what is in this book—especially chapter 10—comes from that conversation as I've thought through what is being said and how that interacts with the Bible.

A fourth reason for my writing this book, as I'll demonstrate in chapter 1, is that the church is in serious decline, perhaps unlike any time in America's past. Not only are vast numbers of people unchurched, but a number of Christians are dropping out of church. And many of these are spiritually vibrant people who feel that their church experience is doing them and their families more harm than good. I believe that new-model churches could offer a viable answer to this dilemma.

Who Should Read This Book?

Every church is a model, whether it likes it or not. Church models are all about how we do church, and every church does church some way. So this book is for all churchgoing Christians. It will help lead pastors who are church planters and revitalizers and their teams think through what they're doing as they wrestle with and develop their church models. Their people will have both questions about and objections to what they're doing, and they will need to provide their people with biblically based, carefully thought-through answers.

However, more specifically, this information is for the people who make up their congregations. It can help them understand what is happening. Consequently, this book is must reading for those congregations that are going through church renewal or church planting. Every congregation is made up of several groups of people who relate to change and new models in different ways. The wise church in general and its leadership in particular will take time to help these people understand the reasons their church does what it does. The following presents four congregational responses to change. As you read through them, determine which category best describes you.

1. The *early adopters* are people who are looking for change and are glad to see it when it happens.
2. The *middle adopters* are slower to move toward change. They are often the majority in the church and tend to be cautious and slightly skeptical. They like to sit back and see what happens. However, given enough time, they adjust to and eventually embrace change.
3. The *late adopters* are highly change resistant and are the last ones in the church to embrace change.
4. The *never adopters* refuse to adopt change and are most vocal about it. They represent only a minority in most churches but make enough noise that people think they are a majority.

Okay, now you know the categories. Which group did you most identify with? More important, what are the implications? For example, if you're a never adopter, why are you reading this book? Isn't your mind already made up? I sure hope not. Perhaps it will give you some insight into what is taking place in the church world early in the twenty-first century.

All of these people ask and need answers for their questions about how to do church. And I've written this book to supply those answers for all four groups. I must confess that I don't hold out a lot of hope for the never adopters. My experience with them has been that they operate more on emotions than facts. Emotionally their mind is already made up. My hope, if you're a never adopter, is that you'll give this book a chance and read it through.

I encourage pastors and all who are leading ministries to give their people a copy of this book. It will save them countless hours of explaining why they're doing what they're doing and hopefully protect them from a lot of grief over what they're doing.

Finally, this book is for seminarians and others who are preparing for ministry. It's important to the future of their ministries that they think through the issues of this book so that they know why they're doing what they're doing and can at the very least articulate the reasons they minister in the context of a particular model, whether it is traditional or contemporary. There will be occasions when they will need to defend their model. And now is the time to think it through.

My Perspective

While it is impossible to approach any topic from a neutral position, I will attempt to do so in this book. I have pastored two traditional churches and one church plant that was slightly more contemporary than traditional. Currently I attend Lake Pointe Church, a contemporary church in Rockwall, Texas, that has recently added a traditional (classic) worship service. Thus I have interests in and respect both ways of doing church. I'm convinced that there is much to learn from both sides about doing church in the twenty-first century.

Furthermore, you must understand that I live outside the life and context of your church. I don't attend your church, so I'm not wrapped up in its politics. While this book might describe your church to a T, I didn't write this book specifically about your church, nor do I have some proverbial ax to grind with a particular group in your church. Thus I hope to address these issues from an objective position.

It's not important whether I or anyone else is traditional or contemporary in our approach to doing church. What is important is what the Bible teaches or doesn't teach on these matters. My authority is the Bible. I'm classically trained as a theologian, thus I have attempted in this book to use Scripture and its biblical theology as a sieve or grid through which I pass what the new models are doing and saying about ministry, along with the responses of their critics. I believe that both sides would agree with my approach. Since a person's background, experience, and preference tend to color the approach he or she prefers for doing church, this book will attempt to focus more on what Scripture says or doesn't say about how we do church today and in the future. (It's interesting that what Scripture doesn't say has vast ramifications about how we do church, as you will see.)

Where You Are Going

Finally, I've divided this work into two parts. Part 1 addresses our changing times. The first chapter asks, Who is changing? It explores the following answers: churches, the unchurched, and those in cults and religious groups. Chapter 2 supplies five answers to the question, Why are the churches changing? And chapter 3 presents the basic arguments for why churches should not change.

Part 2 seeks to provide the reader with the information that he or she needs to make wise decisions about new-paradigm churches. It consists of seven chapters. Chapter 4, "Doing Church," presents a hermeneutic for interpreting the biblical passages on doing church. Chapter 5, "The Changing Church," provides the reader with a biblical theology of change, seeking to answer the question, What does the Bible say about change? Chapter 6, "The Connecting Church," provides a theology of culture and answers the questions, What does the Bible say about culture? How should culture affect the church? Chapter 7, "Defining Church," provides a definition for the local church, which is necessary to answer questions about the legitimacy of church models. Chapter 8, "The Serving Church," provides the reader with Jesus's and Paul's teaching on the church's need to serve and not be served. It closes with an example of such a modern-day church. Chapter 9, "The Thinking Church," returns to the thoughts in chapter 3 and interacts with the critics' arguments against the new-paradigm churches, applying the material in chapters 4–7. Finally, chapter 10, "The Strategizing Church," comes from the point of view that God doesn't endorse any particular church model. It provides a process for developing new church models.

Part 1

Changing Times

Who Is Changing?

Churches Are Changing

The question in the title of this chapter is important because the answer affects increasingly how a growing number of churches do church—whether they stay with an older model or search for and embrace newer ways of doing church. The answer is twofold. First, America's churches are changing—some for the better, many for the worse. Second, America's unchurched and those in cults and religious groups are growing and thus changing. We'll look first at America's changing church landscape. Next, we'll address the growing unchurched population along with those who make up the cults and non-Christian religious groups. Finally, we'll see how a growing number of churches are responding to all this change.

The Changing Church

Churches are changing but not necessarily for the better. If the typical church were to go to a hospital's emergency room, the attending physician would likely admit it to the hospital and put it on life support. Churches all across America are struggling. Some are plateaued and in decline, while others are in the last stages of dying.

Plateaued and Declining

Though some people don't like to admit it, the local church is an organization as well as an organism. Consequently, like other organizations, such as businesses, countries, and even people's relationships, churches experience a beginning, some initial growth, and in time a plateau. And if something doesn't change the situation quickly, they will then begin to decline and eventually die. I refer to this as an organization's life cycle.

The Life Cycle of a Church

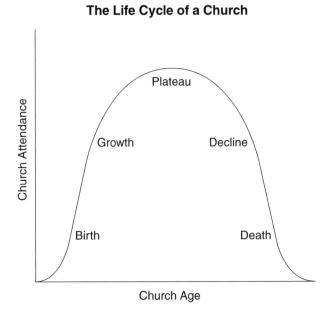

So where might one place the church on the life cycle? Win Arn wrote in the late 1980s that four out of five churches are plateaued or declining.[1] That figure would represent 80 percent of America's churches. My research, as cited in my book *Advanced Strategic Planning*, indicates that this is still the case today and that it is true of evangelical as well as mainline churches.[2] For example, attendance in Southern Baptist churches began to level off in the late 1980s.[3]

At the same time, the number of young people going into the ministry is in decline. Tiara Ellis writes that in 1975 as many as 24 percent of clergy were thirty-five years old or younger. However, in 1999 only 7 percent were thirty-five or younger, and a growing number of these were women.[4]

Dying

A significant number of churches across America are dying. Win Arn observed that, in the late 1980s, 3,500 to 4,000 churches died per year.[5] Church sociologist Lyle Schaller writes, "An estimated 30,000 congregations ceased to exist sometime during the 1980s."[6] An article in *Ministry* predicted that, of the 350,000 churches in America, as many as 100,000 would close their doors.[7]

The Unchurched, Cults, and Religious Groups

The number of unchurched people is changing, but not the way we want. Instead of declining, their numbers are growing. And the same is true of the number of people involved in cults and other non-Christian religious organizations.

Unchurched People

Before looking at the increase in the number of unchurched people, I must define what I mean by *unchurched*. George Gallup has been a leader in researching unchurched people in America. He defines the unchurched as "those who are not members of a church or have not attended services in the previous six months other than for special religious holidays, weddings, funerals or the like."[8] (Early in the twenty-first century, this definition is beginning to change slightly as a growing number of committed Christians are dropping out of church. I'll say more about this below.)

George Barna indicates that the number of unchurched Americans has increased 92 percent in the last thirteen years. In 1991 there were thirty-nine million compared with seventy-five million unchurched in 2004.[9] As of March 2005 the Barna Group shows that one-third of all adults, or 34 percent, are unchurched.[10]

Barna states that 35 percent of Mosaics, 30 percent of Busters, 49 percent of Boomers, and 54 percent of Builders attend church on any given Sunday.[11] The following chart shows how many are unchurched.

Generation	Birth Years	Percentage Unchurched
Builders	1927–1945	46%
Boomers	1946–1964	51%
Busters	1965–1983	70%
Mosaics	1984–2002	65%

I'm a little surprised that so many of the Builder generation are unchurched (46 percent). After World War II, they filled America's churches and made up its most faithful people in terms of attendance and giving. It would appear that a number of them have dropped out of church, possibly due to health and other issues.

Unfortunately, the Busters and the Mosaics, the future of America's churches as well as the future of the nation, are essentially unchurched (65–70 percent). This doesn't bode well for the future church in America.

Barna indicates that the largest number of unchurched people live in the Northeast (44 percent). Thirty-three percent live in the West, and 32 percent in the Midwest. The least number of unchurched live in the South (26 percent).[12]

Northeast	West	Midwest	South
44% unchurched	33% unchurched	32% unchurched	26% unchurched

Most demographers have noted that more women than men attend church. Cynthia Woolever's research indicates that 61 percent of women are churched as compared to 39 percent of men.[13] Barna states that, although men make up slightly less than half the national population, they constitute 55 percent of the unchurched.[14]

You would naturally think that men are to blame for their nonparticipation in church. However, David Murrow writes in *Why Men Hate Going to Church* that while some men just choose not to go, today's church is also culpable because it has developed a culture that is driving men away. This culture values female qualities over those of males. For example, many of today's churches value safety over risk, stability over change, preservation over expansion, and predictability over adventure. Thus in his book Murrow does not call men back to church but the church back to men.[15] Today's churches must realize that Jesus, his disciples, and the early church didn't have any problem attracting men. They developed a culture that included such characteristics as challenge (Matt. 4:18–19), commitment (v. 20), conviction (Acts 20:22–24), and risk (Acts 4:29), as well as a number of other qualities that likely attracted men. If our churches are to make a difference in the future, it is imperative that they address this issue!

Barna states that in 2004 more than one half (54 percent) of unchurched adults considered themselves to be Christian. Whereas in 2000, 11 percent professed to be born-again Christians (meaning that they have made a personal commitment to Christ and believe they have eternal salvation through Jesus's death and resurrection).[16] Thus somewhere between 11 and 54 percent of those who are unchurched may know Christ as Savior. Regardless, the number of unchurched Christians or those professing to be Christians is growing, and an increasing number is dropping out of the church.

Professing Christians	Nonprofessing Christians
54% of unchurched	46% of unchurched

Born-Again Christians	Not Born-Again Christians
11% of unchurched	89% of unchurched

In his research dated October 10, 2005, Barna states that twenty million unchurched people are Christians. He writes, "We found that while some people leave the local church and fall away from God altogether, there is a much larger segment of Americans who are currently leaving churches precisely because they want more of God in their life but cannot get what they need from a local church."[17] Many of us have assumed that those who drop out are mostly unbelievers or carnal Christians. We learn from Barna that some are carnal Christians, but a growing proportion (perhaps the majority) are deeply committed believers. What a sad commentary on the state of the American church! These Christians are leaving church because the experience hasn't furthered their commitment to God. It would appear that a significant number—possibly a majority—of our struggling churches sprinkled all across America represent a lukewarm rather than a vibrant Christianity that is doing more harm than good to those who attend them. Could it be that a growing number of Christians who want to mature in their faith and commitment to the Savior are better off leaving their churches and looking for some alternative ministries, such as those found in the parachurch sector?

The Barna Group and George Gallup gathered their information by polling people through self-identification or self-reporting surveys. Perhaps someone has called you on the phone or sent you a survey through the mail. To what degree should we trust this information?

Another pollster, Lou Harris, acknowledges, "It should be noted that church attendance is notoriously over-reported as a socially desirable activity, so true attendance figures are surely lower than those reported here."[18] And Barry Kosmin, codirector of the 2001 American Religious Identification Survey, notes in USA Today: "Leadership of all faiths exaggerate or manufacture their numbers."[19]

C. Kirk Hadaway and a team of sociologists have challenged the accuracy of the polls. In the article "What the Polls Don't Show," they addressed Gallup's earlier finding that 60 percent of Americans were unchurched. Their research indicated that 80 percent of Protestants and 72 percent of Catholics are unchurched. They argued that poll respondents in self-reports substantially overstate their church attendance.[20]

I have taught at Dallas Theological Seminary in Dallas, Texas, for the last twenty-five years. I've also consulted with churches in the Dallas–Fort Worth area over the past ten to fifteen years. Not only is Dallas–Fort Worth located in the Bible Belt, the two cities are "the buckle" of the Bible Belt. Even in such a place, my findings agree with Hadaway and his team. Some surveys in the area would also back this up. One survey of Plano, Texas, located north of Dallas, found that 74 percent of its residents were unchurched.[21] Another survey in Arlington, Texas (slightly west of Dallas), estimates that 74 percent of its 270,000 residents don't attend church.[22]

So how accurate are the pollsters' statistics? I believe that people do over report such things as church attendance and that the pollsters' figures are off significantly, and you would be wise to consider this when you look at the statistics I've cited above. The situation is likely worse than what the figures show. My experience is that the 80 percent unchurched figure is probably the more accurate one. This means that today America is widely unchurched, reflecting a post-Christian status.

Those Involved in Cults and Non-Christian Religions

Not only have the ranks of unchurched people increased, but many cults and religious organizations are growing as well. One group that is growing and prospering is the Mormons. This was reported in *U.S. News and World Report*:

> Today the Church of Jesus Christ of Latter-Day Saints, better known as the Mormon Church, is one of the world's richest and fastest-growing religious movements. Since World War II, its ranks have quadrupled to more than 8.3 million members worldwide. With 4.5 million U.S. members, Mormonism already outnumbers Presbyterians and Episcopalians combined. If current trends hold, by some estimates they will number 250 million worldwide by 2080 and surpass all but the Roman Catholic Church among Christian bodies.[23]

The *Yearbook of American and Canadian Churches* reports that the Mormon Church has tripled from 1,789,175 in 1965 to 5,113,409 in 2001.[24]

Cults

Mormons

1965	2001
1,789,175	5,113,409

The *Dallas Morning News* reported the following in 2002:

> For the first time, the Church of Jesus Christ of Latter-day Saints is reported within the five largest churches in the United States, according to the National Council of Churches 2002 *Yearbook of American and Canadian Churches*.
>
> "This ranking represents a very brisk increase in membership for a church with a relatively brief history," said the Rev. Eileen W. Lindner, the yearbook's editor. The Latter-Day Saints were organized in 1830.[25]

The Jehovah's Witnesses have also experienced tremendous growth. The *Yearbook of American and Canadian Churches* reports that from 1988 to 2001 this group increased from 330,358 to 990,340.[26]

Cults

Jehovah's Witnesses

1988	2001
330,358	990,340

Another religious group that has taken root in America and is growing is Islam. According to a study from the Hartford Seminary, Muslim mosques are springing up in cities and suburbs across America.[27]

This same report indicates that Muslim growth has exceeded that of the Mormon Church:

> According to the FACT survey, the number of mosques in the United States increased 42 percent between 1990 and 2000, compared with a 12 percent average increase among old-line Protestant, Catholic, and Orthodox groups. The Latter-Day Saints and Assemblies of God congregations exceeded the evangelical average, but fell short of the growth in the number of mosques.[28]

Finally, this study indicates that American Muslims are eager to become full and accepted participants in the mainstream of American cultural, political, and religious life.

Non-Christian Religious Groups

Islam

Years	Percent Increase
1990–2000	42%

Much the same can be said of the spread of Islam in Western Europe. I was watching the funeral of Pope John Paul II at the Vatican on CNN. In passing, the reporter mentioned that not far from the Vatican is a large Muslim mosque. He added that currently in England more Muslims attend a mosque than Anglicans attend church.

Another fast-growing non-Christian group is the Buddhists. They grew 109.5 percent from 1990 to 2001.[29]

Non-Christian Religious Groups

Buddhists

Years	Percent Increase
1990–2001	109.5%

A third fast-growing group is Hindus. They grew 237.4 percent from 1990 to 2001.[30]

Non-Christian Religious Groups

Hindus

Years	Percent Increase
1990–2001	237.4%

By far the fastest-growing non-Christian group is the Wiccans. These self-proclaimed witches have grown from 8,000 in 1990 to 134,000 in 2001. This is an astounding growth rate of 1,575 percent.[31]

Non-Christian Groups

Wiccans

Years	Percent Increase
1990–2001	1,575%

What does all this mean? I've shown that churches are changing, mostly for the worse, and that some of the cults and non-Christian religious groups are growing. Some interpret this as evidence that America is strictly a post-Christian nation with little to no interest in spiritual matters. I would agree that America is quickly becoming post-Christian, but I arrive at a different conclusion when it comes to the nation's interest in spiritual matters. I believe that the information above is evidence that people are most interested in spirituality, but they aren't looking to today's typical neighborhood church for answers to their spiritual questions. They view these churches as out of touch and thus irrelevant to them, and they conclude that the church doesn't have answers to their questions, at least not the questions they're currently asking.

I use the term *spiritual* very broadly. In the mid-twentieth century, when most people used the term *spiritual*, they were using it in the context of the Bible and Christianity. Today it includes far more than that. For example, I was flying back to Dallas from a trip to California. A woman from Colorado sat next to me on the plane. We struck up a conversation that eventually moved to spiritual matters. She explained to me that she was a spiritual person who was interested in spiritual things, which for her meant crystals and New Age thought.

I think it's clear that now more than ever the church must not bury its proverbial head in the sand. Now is the time for the church to reach out as never before and demonstrate that it is very much aware of what is going on around it and has relevant answers to life's dilemmas. The church is the hope of the world, and it's time for it to make a difference in our world. But one might wonder if the typical American church is even aware of what is taking place all around it and what the implications are. Thom Rainer summarizes the situation best: "America is clearly becoming less Christian, less evangelized, and less churched. Yet too many of those in our churches seem oblivious to this reality."[32]

New Church Models

While the majority of the nation's churches are struggling with decline and death, a growing number of churches are looking for answers to the problem of declining congregations. Established churches as well as new church plants want more than anything to make a difference to a lost and dying world. And they're not willing to sit idly by with their hands in their pockets and watch churches decline.

A growing number of church leaders have become disillusioned with the way church has been done in the past. Admonitions of "If it ain't broke don't fix it" and "We just need to work harder" are falling on deaf ears. Many of these leaders respond, "Can't they see that it is broke?" and "Working harder isn't working smarter!"

Actually the problem isn't with the older model of church. There was a time when this model of church reached people, and it may still reach some people in some places today and in the future. The problem is that people and their preferences change, rendering older models obsolete—at least for the time being. I heard one Christian leader, who will remain anonymous, put it this way: "I know that my children want nothing to do with the form of church and Christianity that I practice." Thus the old saying, "If the horse is dead, dismount," applies.

Some churches *are* changing. They don't look like the churches of the twentieth century, and they do church differently. And we have to ask if this is okay.

Before I address this question, we must explore why all this is happening, which is the topic of the next chapter, and what many critics of all this change are saying about the new-model churches, the topic of chapter 3.

Questions for Reflection and Discussion

1. Before reading this chapter, were you aware that churches were in decline and that the unchurched and non-Christian religious groups were growing? If not, why not?

2. Were you aware that an increasing number of church "drop-outs" are committed Christians who feel that remaining in their churches is harmful to their faith? What does this say about America's churches? Is this the case at your church?

3. Where is your church on the organizational life cycle pictured at the beginning of this chapter? Why is it where it is?

4. If your church is plateaued or dying, what will you do about it? Have you considered more leadership training or using a church consultant? Why or why not?

Why Are Churches Changing?

The Buck Stops Here!

Often we Americans find it difficult to accept the blame for our mistakes. Instead, we follow the time-honored tradition of passing the buck. We glance from side to side, looking for someone else to blame as we state for the record, "It's not my fault!"

The story is told of President Harry Truman who during difficult times placed a placard on his desk that read, "The buck stops here!" I suspect that some of the leaders of the new-model churches have followed suit and placed a similar placard on their desks.

Chapter 1 has surfaced the serious problem that confronts the institutional American church early in the twenty-first century—it's basically declining while the number of unchurched people along with some of the cults and non-Christian groups are growing. The temptation is to look quickly for a solution, since the souls of people are at stake. However, we would be wise to pause and explore some of the reasons for this decline. We must ask why churches are changing. Most often, discovering the reasons for our problems leads to finding solutions to those problems and, in this case, may help to guide the development of future church models as well as to discern good and bad church models. This chapter will address two issues. First, we'll look at some of the reasons people who need to be reached for the Savior aren't attending our churches. Next, we'll examine the churches, those whom Christ has commissioned to reach these people, to see where they may be at fault.

Why Americans Are Not Attending Church

America is a democracy, and the First Amendment to the Constitution guarantees every American the freedom to worship as he or she pleases. Unlike countries that embrace Islam and insist that their people hold to the Muslim faith, Americans are free to attend church when and where they choose or not to attend at all. In short, they can take religion or leave it. So most Americans vote with their feet. If they feel that church is addressing their needs—spiritual or otherwise—they attend; if not, they walk away. The following will address three core reasons why a growing number are opting for walking away early in the twenty-first century.

People Think Differently

One reason many people don't attend or no longer attend church is that they think differently than do people in the typical church. More than one-half of America's congregations were established prior to World War II.[1] While there is nothing wrong with being an older congregation, far too many think and act as if they were still living in the period before World War II. That would be okay if we were actually living in pre–World War II America. However, this is the twenty-first century, and this country and the way it thinks has changed light-years over the last sixty to seventy years.

How are we different now? The typical pre–World War II person lived in a monocultural world. America was largely white, Anglo-Saxon, and Protestant or Catholic. Travel was difficult, and few people traveled or conducted business overseas. Consequently, Americans were not all that familiar with people of other countries and religions. Modernism was the predominant worldview, and most people placed their faith for a better world in science and education. Only a few had access to computers, which were housed in large air-conditioned buildings. The typical unchurched unbeliever was often a young college student who would challenge the church with the question, Does God exist?

That world no longer exists. Today's person lives in a multicultural world where CNN can transport him or her to any place on the globe at the click of a remote control. Postmodernism has challenged modernism as the prevalent worldview, and many young people feel that hope for the future lies more with the poets and artists than the scientists and educators. Most people have their own computers and carry them with them—mine weighs only three pounds. Young, unchurched adults are asking a different question: Which God is real?

The Internet and other sources have exposed the average American to various non-Christian faiths, such as Judaism, Buddhism, Hinduism, and Islam. Of those engaged in religious activities online, 50 percent use the Internet to research other faiths.[2] Many Builders, who were young prior to and following World War II, have yet to purchase a computer, and many of their churches are set up to answer so-called real-life questions that people are no longer asking, so these churches are set up for failure. The majority of Americans are responding to the traditional church's invitation to "come meet with us on our terms" with a polite (sometimes not so polite) "no thanks."

Faith Is No Longer Tied to the Church

Another reason people no longer attend church is that their faith is inextricably tied neither to the church nor to its leadership, as was true for the Builder generation in the early and mid-twentieth century. Early in 1990 Gallup discovered that an overwhelming number of church attenders as well as the unchurched believed that people "should arrive at their religious beliefs independent of any church or synagogue." Further, one could be a good Christian or Jew without being a part of any Christian or Jewish faith community.[3]

How important is the clergy to the faith process? Whereas Gallup found that 67 percent of the populace had confidence in the clergy in 1985, that figure dropped 13 percentage points to 54 percent between 1992 and 1995.[4] The tendency among the Builder generation was to trust the clergy until they gave them some reason not to, which happened late in the 1980s and 1990s when a number of clergy confessed to moral lapses and other problems. The tendency among the younger generations in general and the Busters in particular has been not to start out by trusting clergy. The clergy have to earn their trust.

Does this mean that these people are upset with or even angry at the institution of the church? Not necessarily. When asked why they no longer attend church, many unchurched felt that it simply wasn't that important, while 34 percent said they were just too busy.[5] And many others are looking elsewhere for answers to their questions about spiritual matters because they believe the church is answering questions that most of them aren't asking.

As is so often the case, when it comes to church attendance, Americans are individualists who pride themselves in their personal autonomy and can do what they want. Wade Clark Roof and William McKinney write: "Typically Americans view religious congregations as gatherings of individuals who have chosen to be together, in institutions of their own making and over which they hold control—fostering what sometimes, in the eyes of observers from other countries, appears as 'churchless Christianity.'"[6]

The issue is one of authority. Where lies the authority for what we believe and do? Far too many Americans are individualists who are convinced that "religious authority lies in the believer—not in the church, not in the Bible, despite occasional claims of infallibility and inerrancy on the part of some."[7]

Another factor is one's prior exposure to church. The Builder generation and many of the Boomer generation grew up with some exposure to the church, especially in the South. The general expectation among the Builders and their parents was that one went to church on Sunday mornings. Many of the Boomer generation attended church when they were young because their Builder parents took them. Yet many opted to walk away once they graduated from high school.

In contrast, a large number of the Busters and Mosaics have rarely attended church, if at all. Their question for the established church is, Why should I attend your church when there are so many other things that I could be doing? For many, attending church, except on Easter, Christmas, and for an occasional wedding or funeral, isn't on their list of options. It's imperative that today's churches give good answers to the younger generation's question, not just, What's good enough for us is good enough for you! or We've always done it that way! This kind of response seems foolish to today's young people.

An important current movement among Christians is either dropping out of church altogether or adding other alternatives to church gatherings because they view traditional church involvement as harmful to their faith development. I commented briefly on this in chapter 1. In one of his studies George Barna addresses what he believes will be a massive reshaping of America's faith community. He notes that there are more than twenty million adults who have dropped out of church, not because they've lost interest in spiritual matters or are disconnecting from God, but because they want *more* of God in their lives. These are believers who are less interested in attending church and more interested in *being* the church. Barna believes that the local church is the primary form of faith for about two-thirds of America's adults in 2005. He projects, however, that the local church will lose about half of its current "market share" to other forms of faith expression by the year 2025. He goes so far as to believe that this movement of finding alternatives to church involvement could become known as the Third Great Awakening in America's history.[8]

Sunday Morning Is No Longer Sacred

A third reason people no longer attend church is that Sunday morning is no longer sacred. The church reached its highest attendance levels between 1954 and 1962, according to Gallup's statistics. For the Builder generation, church attendance offered respectability. Going to church was what proper, middle-class suburban people did on Sunday mornings, especially in the South. Participation in church concurred with an emphasis on the family. It was also associated with patriotism and a strong belief in government and most major institutions. During this time in some parts of the United States, American culture also became largely a churched culture. Church is what many people in the South and some parts of the North did on Sunday mornings. Some cities had "blue laws" that prohibited stores from opening on Sundays as well. For some people church was the only thing to do on Sunday mornings besides sleep in.

However, all that has changed in most of America. Sunday mornings are sacred no longer, and a number of rivals have surfaced to compete with the church for the hearts and souls of the American citizenry on Sunday. With the repeal of the blue laws, stores can be open on Sunday as well as the other six days of the week. This means that many people have to or choose to work on Sunday.

I was pastoring my second church when the blue laws were repealed in Texas in the 1980s. I didn't support the blue laws, naively thinking that the church could hold its own, even if stores were open. However, I came to understand the impact on the church when one of my members told me that he wouldn't be around much on Sundays anymore because his store would be open and he had to work to keep his job.

Another rival is sports, both participant and spectator. Early in the second half of the twentieth century, only professional football and later basketball competed with churches for customers on Sunday. At the end of the twentieth century and into the twenty-first century, all that has changed. On a Sunday in December in Dallas, one can attend a Dallas Cowboys football game, a Dallas Mavericks basketball game, or a Dallas Stars hockey game. If one prefers to actively participate in a sport, there's touch football, softball, and numerous soccer leagues—all on Sunday. Other favorite Sunday activities are jogging around area lakes or working out at a local fitness center for weight control and other health-related benefits.

My community is a great example. Not far from my house in Dallas is White Rock Lake, the largest man-made lake within a city's limits in America. When I leave for church on Sunday morning, usually there are numerous sailboats darting around on the lake as well as people jogging or biking on a track that circles the lake. Right up the street is the Dallas Arboretum, a large flower and plant garden, where many go to participate in events called Dallas Blooms. In addition to all this, a well-maintained public golf course is one-half mile in the opposite direction, not to mention two Starbucks within a mile of my residence. All of this coupled with the Dallas Cowboys or any professional football team on cable television makes it difficult for our Dallas churches to draw people. The competition is not other churches but all the leisure activities that are available on Sunday morning.

I contend that while the institutional church of the twenty-first century must compete with these rivals and others as well, it can't win the competition for the hearts and minds of secular Americans, especially men. It will lose every time. For example, would a typical Dallasite rather go to a struggling, dwindling church on Sunday and listen to what often is a boring sermon or stay at home and watch the Dallas Cowboys, Mavericks, or Stars? Many opt for the latter or go to a shopping mall. Others see Sunday as a chance for a little time with the family at the beach, an opportunity to put in a little overtime at the office, or a chance to clean up the yard or catch up on the housekeeping. Congregations would be wise to build relationships with their unchurched friends and invite them to church rather than assume they will come on their own. Often unchurched people value relationships and will consider attending a church when invited by a friend.

Three Core Reasons Americans Aren't Attending Church

- People think differently today.
- A person's faith is no longer tied to the church.
- Sunday morning is no longer sacred.

Where Churches Are at Fault

Donald Messer tells of a cartoon that portrays two young men sitting in the sun, wearing their baseball caps backwards, as is the custom with so many American youth. One looks at the other and remarks, "Somebody ought to invent a cap that would give a guy some shade!"[9] This image is helpful as we think about churches and why so many aren't reaching people. Like the baseball cap, these churches seem to have lost their original mission—"make disciples" (Matt. 28:19–20). There are four ways that the church has its hat on backwards.

Too Slow to Change

A visit to some churches is like a step back in time. If a young person in the early twenty-first century wants to know how they did church in America back in the early to mid-twentieth century, all he or she has to do is visit an established, traditional church in the community. Though few other institutions or organizations reflect those times, you can count on the church to be there. In fact, it's one of the few remaining reminders of European life and culture in America.

Messer compares attending a typical church to experiencing a time warp similar to that found in Michael Crichton's *Jurassic Park*.

Welcome to Jurassic Park Denomination. You are now entering the lost world of the prehistoric past. Our tour begins in the board library. Here we notice two rare species. First the board member always pushing for more exegetical sermons from the Old Testament, the *bron-Torah-saurus*. Next to him you can see this creature's rival, the board member who likes lighter sermons, the *triceratopical*. On the right you can see the board member who loves to study the end times, *velocirapture*. Next, we proceed to the church kitchen. Here we find a board member who loves grazing at potlucks, socials, and outdoor picnics, the *barbequesaurus*.[10]

The real problems lie in the church's methodology or how it "does church," reflected in its particular church model. So many in our churches are convinced that we must conduct church the way we've always done it. As one old-timer (the *traditionsaurus*) put it, "If the organ and the great hymns of the faith were good enough for Jesus and Paul, they must be good enough for us!" Bill Easum writes:

> Like the dinosaur, they [churches] have a voracious appetite. Much of their time, energy, and money is spent foraging for food, so that little time is left to feed the unchurched. . . . Food is everywhere. But many refuse to change their methods and structures to minister to people where they are in ways they can understand. Like the dinosaur, their necks are too stiff or their eyes too nearsighted.[11]

Easum concludes: "Congregations must deal with their stiff necks or their nearsightedness, or go the way of the dinosaur."[12] Some congregations will wake up in time to deal effectively with their situations. Their necks will soften and their eyesight will be corrected. We call this refocusing or revitalizing the church. Others will wake up, but it will be too late. However, too many will never wake up and will simply pass from the scene like the dinosaur.

It is difficult to change. For many the church is the one place you can go and count on it being the same week after week. In the world of work we have to confront changes every other day. However, the gospel argues that our churches must think about others as well as ourselves. A case in point is our youth who are the church's future. In short, no youth, no future. George Barna warns us:

> Faith is just one component in people's lives that helps them to interpret and cope with reality—and it certainly is not the central shaping influence for most people. The data regarding young adults also pose the possibility that churches are losing ground in terms of influence and may need to consider new approaches to making ancient truths more vivid and comprehensible in a technology-drenched, relativistic global community.[13]

The question that every church faces is, What can or must change, and what must never change? The answer is found in one's theology of change. This is the crux of the problem for all churches in general and the American church in particular and is the topic of chapter 5, where I discuss the fact that the church can flex in its forms but not in its functions. Scripture dictates what the church must do (its functions, such as evangelism, worship, biblical teaching) but not how it does it (the forms, such as a contemporary or a traditional worship style). The church must not change its message—if that message is based on the Bible—but the church must rethink how it communicates the biblical message. My experience is that most churches and their leadership, including the clergy, haven't thought this through. And in a time when one of the only constants is change, it's imperative that the church develop and follow a biblical theology of change.

Failure to Take Advantage of Opportunities

Churches that have their hats on backwards neither see nor take advantage of their God-given opportunities. Scripture teaches that God is sovereign over the universe (Acts 4:24–30) and that he uses all events, good or bad, for the good of those who love him and have been called according to his purpose (Rom. 8:28). This means that the various events that take place in people's lives aren't happenstance. When these take place, churches must ask how they can use these events to glorify God and reach out to those who are affected by them.

A case in point is the terrorist attacks on the World Trade Center in New York on September 11, 2001. This tragic event that has changed America in so many ways raises two strategic questions that the church must consider. First, how did the people that the churches are trying to reach (the target) respond to this event? And second, how did the church respond to the people?

The answer to the first question is that a number of people who had never attended or had stopped attending church were in church the following Sunday morning. A Gallup poll reported that 47 percent of adults surveyed September 21–22, 2001, said that they had attended church or synagogue the previous week. This number was the highest since the 1950s.[14] The Barna Research Group reported that 48 percent of adults surveyed in late October and early November of 2001 said they had attended a church service in the last week compared with 42 percent polled earlier between late July and early August.

Barna also noted an increase in concern about the future. In November, 82 percent of the adults that Barna surveyed said they were concerned about the future compared to 73 percent in August.[15] Barna added that the population segment that expressed the most concern was adults thirty-five and younger, among whom nearly nine out of ten expressed their concern.[16] Again, the latter represent not only the future of our nation but the future of our churches.

Social scientists and analysts have discovered that most people turn to religion in times of national crisis and instability. Few evangelical Christians doubt that God used the attacks on September 11 to wake up Americans in general and the churches in particular to people's need for God and the church's role in helping them connect with him. People responded to the crisis as we might expect. Did the church use the opportunity to connect with them for the Savior?

The answer isn't encouraging. Contrary to the Barna report noted above, a Gallup poll conducted from November 8 to 11 revealed that church attendance had dropped from 47 percent in late September to 42 percent, which is practically where it was before the terrorist attacks.[17] According to Gallup, the people who had come immediately after the attack didn't stick.

Regarding his post–September 11 survey, Barna believes that the results indicate that churches failed to help post-attack newcomers connect with or deepen their faith. He explained:

> After the attack, millions of nominally churched or generally irreligious Americans were desperately seeking something that would restore stability and a sense of meaning to life. Fortunately, many of them turned to the church. Unfortunately, few of them experienced anything that was sufficiently life-changing to capture their attention and their allegiance. They tended to appreciate the moments of comfort they received, but were unaware of anything sufficiently unique or beneficial as to redesign their lifestyle to integrate a deeper level of spiritual involvement. Our assessment is that churches succeeded at putting on a friendly face but failed at motivating the vast majority of spiritual explorers to connect with Christ in a more intimate or intense manner.[18]

What we discover is that the church wasn't ready for this tragic event. Like so many others, it was caught by surprise. Unlike so many others, such as firemen, policemen, and the Red Cross, as well as many average citizens, it failed to react well. It didn't use the tragedy strategically for spiritual advantage. The church must learn to respond quickly to traumatic experiences and make a difference. We might argue that emergency-oriented organizations like the New York Fire and Police Departments as well as the Red Cross are prepared for such disasters. Whether or not the church is in decline, it is vital that it become an emergency-oriented organization as well. Regarding the two most recent opportunities (President Bush's faith-based initiatives and the terrorist attack), Barna challenges the church:

> These two events are a wake-up call to church leaders, emphasizing the particular need to enhance their efforts in the areas of outreach and discipleship. We may never again have such grand opportunities to reach the nation for Christ—but then, we may have an even greater opportunity tomorrow. How many churches have leaders and believers who are poised to take advantage of such a pending opportunity?[19]

Barna isn't entirely correct about never again having grand opportunities to reach people. For example, in August and September 2005 two hurricanes—Katrina and Rita—brought devastation to those along the Gulf Coast in general and Louisiana, Mississippi, Alabama, and parts of Texas in particular. This catastrophe exceeded that of 9/11 in New York and presented two more grand opportunities for the church to reach people, especially along the coast where it hit. So far churches have responded well in and around the states that were hit so hard. For example, a number of churches in the Dallas–Fort Worth Metroplex have opened up their facilities to feed and house large numbers of refugees from the hurricanes. Churches in the same area have been noticeably full on Sunday mornings. So people are looking to the churches again for some answers. But did we learn anything from September 11 that helped us have a greater impact in September 2005?

The growing response to the AIDS crisis is another promising move on the part of some churches to be more involved in catastrophic issues that get lost people's attention and draw them to church. Pastor Rick Warren of Saddleback Church in Southern California and his wife, Kay, are attempting to rally our nation's evangelical churches in particular to address and reach out to those in America and abroad who suffer from the AIDS pandemic. This is a first for America's evangelical churches, who historically have avoided such social issues to focus more on the nation's so-called spiritual issues. In the past such social issues have been under the purview of the American mainline churches that tend to be more liberal in their theology. If more evangelical churches begin to address these issues, they will provide help for those struggling with the problems as well as a theology to go along with it. With the evangelical churches moving into their areas of concern and ministry, I wonder what need there will be in the future for America's liberal churches? What will they have to offer that the evangelical church doesn't?

Lack of Value of Evangelism

In the conclusion to chapter 1, I quoted Thom Rainer who warned, "America is clearly becoming less Christian, less evangelized, and less churched. Yet too many of those in our churches seem oblivious to this reality."[20] The problem is that the overwhelming majority of American churches aren't committed to evangelism. My experience as a consultant working with churches from coast to coast is that evangelism is a dying value in America.

After the terrorist attacks and the resulting interest of many people in spiritual matters, church leaders hoped that the church would experience a renewed emphasis on evangelism. However, a Barna Research Group survey found that statistics before and after the terrorist attacks concerning those who have made a "personal commitment to Jesus Christ that is still important in your life today" were identical at 68 percent.[21] And we must not assume that the lost are mostly unchurched. In a December 17, 2001, survey, the Barna Group states, "Forty-one percent of the adults who attend Christian church services in a typical week are not born-again Christians—meaning they have not embraced Jesus Christ as Savior."[22] It would seem obvious that the church has somehow fallen down on the job of evangelism even within its own ranks.

In the spring of 2001, Rainer put together a team from The Billy Graham School of Missions, Evangelism, and Church Growth at Southern Baptist Theological Seminary in Louisville, Kentucky. The goal was to conduct research on the unchurched in America. The team came to one startling conclusion on the church's role in evangelism. Rainer writes: "Our research team has come to similar conclusions. Less than 4 percent of churches in America meet our criteria to be an effective evangelistic church. Only one person is reached for Christ each year for every eighty-five church members in America."[23] Perhaps an analogy would help. Assume for a moment that you own an insurance company with eighty-five salespersons. How long would you be in business if they sold only one policy per year? This may give us a better picture of the reason so many churches are going out of business.

Baptists, who have been known for their evangelism, have traditionally had a strong passion to reach our lost and dying world. How are they doing at the beginning of a new century? Barna reports at the end of 2001 that "just four out of ten adults attending a Baptist church shared their faith in Christ with a non-believer in the past year—less than the proportion of adherents of many other denominations."[24] This is most troubling to me because I'm currently a member and elder in a Baptist church outside Dallas.

For much of my life as a Christian, I've attended and at times pastored a Bible Church. A significant number of students who attend such schools as Moody Bible Institute, Multnomah School of the Bible, and Dallas Theological Seminary, graduate and minister in churches that over the years have become part of the Bible Church or Teaching Church Movement. The churches that make up this movement are popularly known primarily for their sound exposition of the Bible. Word has it, if you want to learn the Bible, go to a Bible Church.

How are the Bible Churches doing in evangelism? My experience is that they're not doing well. I know of some that have gone for years with no conversions. This is surprising because you would think that a movement that values teaching and studying the Bible would be strong in obeying the Bible. This doesn't seem to be the case. One friend who was a pastor of a Bible Church in Dallas attempted to introduce change that included targeting and evangelizing lost people. The former pastors of this church have been teaching the Bible for over a half century. He showed me a letter from a complaining member who wrote that the most important thing is to teach the Bible! According to the very same Bible, that member was wrong. The mission of the church, according to Matthew 28:19–20, is to make disciples, and that includes evangelism as well as other functions. However, I suspect that many churches hold views similar to those of this Bible Church.

One of the reasons churches aren't doing evangelism is that their pastors neither do evangelism nor value it. Barna reports, "Just 12 percent of senior pastors say they have the spiritual gift of leadership, only 8 percent say they have the gift of evangelism; in contrast, two-thirds say they have the gift of teaching or preaching."[25] A person doesn't have to have the evangelistic gift to share his or her faith. However, most often those with the gift of evangelism value evangelism and are impassioned to share their faith.

We've looked at some who aren't sharing their faith and were unpleasantly surprised. When we look at those who are sharing their faith, we are pleasantly surprised. Again the Barna Research Group supplies this information: "After exploring the religious life of adults attending a variety of Protestant churches, only three types of churches—Pentecostal, Assemblies of God, and nondenominational churches—had a majority of adherents who had shared their faith in Christ with a non-Christian

in the past year."[26] This is important because many of these believers
are charismatic in persuasion. And those who tend to pride themselves
in not being charismatic tend to look down their noses at charismatics
for their so-called theological naïveté. However, there's a huge difference
between being theologically naive and not obeying the clear teaching
of Scripture.

It will be impossible for the church of Jesus Christ to revive itself
and make a difference for the Savior in this world if it doesn't obey the
Great Commission and share its faith. It is imperative that churches
face this issue and commit to their God-intended mission.

Not Recruiting Gifted Leaders

I said above that the church is the hope of the world. What I didn't
say is that leadership is the hope of the church. Everything rises or falls
with leadership. I was talking recently with someone who ministers
with a large denomination. His job is to work with the pastors of the
denomination's churches, and they are facing the problem of not having
enough pastors with a leadership gift. Many are good managers but
not good leaders. My experience in working with churches as well is
that if the senior pastor doesn't have a leadership gift, then often the
church moves to a plateau and eventually slips into decline.

Seminaries aren't helping the situation. They tend to be strong in
such areas as Bible and theology, and these are critical; however, their
pastoral ministries departments tend to focus on preaching, not leadership. I'm not saying that preaching the Bible isn't important, because of
course it is. But so is leadership. I have watched many gifted teachers
graduate from seminary hoping to teach at a Bible college or seminary.
The problem is that these positions are rare, and one must have at least
a Ph.D. to teach at most seminaries for accreditation purposes. Thus
these men drift into churches where they can exercise their teaching
gifts from the pulpit. And they are able to clearly expound where the
church is supposed to be going, but they're not able to lead it there.

Frequently I get questionnaires from various churches that are con-
sidering one of our Dallas graduates as a future pastor. They ask lots
of good questions about their character, how they did in school, their
knowledge of the Bible and theology, and how well they preach. Few
ever ask about their leadership gifts and abilities. Again the church is
caught not asking the more important questions. Remember, the church
rises or falls with godly, gifted leadership from top to bottom.

Where Churches Are at Fault

- Churches are too slow to change their methods.
- Churches have failed to take advantage of their opportunities.
- Churches don't value evangelism.
- Churches aren't recruiting gifted leaders.

Questions for Reflection and Discussion

1. What is the average age of your congregation? Do you have both young and older people? If so, what are some ways in which younger people in your church think differently than older people? What are some ways younger people in your community think differently than those in your church? Has this affected the church's ministry in general and outreach in particular? If so, how?
2. Would you say that the faith of the people in your community is tied to the church? If yes, how so? If no, explain. What do people in your community think about pastors? Do they tend to trust or distrust them? If you don't know, ask an unchurched friend this question.
3. What do people in your community do on Sunday mornings or at times when most churches meet? Do many choose to attend church? If not, why? If you don't know, why don't you know?
4. Where is your church in terms of change? Would a visit to your church be a Jurassic Park experience? What can you do about this? What will you do?
5. Does your church typically take advantage of its God-given opportunities to reach people? How did it respond to the terrorist attacks on September 11, 2001? Why? How did it respond to Hurricanes Katrina and Rita in September 2005? Why?
6. Is your church committed to evangelism? Is your pastor strong in evangelism? Is evangelism an actual core value of your church? How do you know? Is it reaching lost people? If so, how many? If not, why not? If not, what will you do about this?
7. Does your pastor have a leadership gift? If yes, how do you know? If no, how do you know? If the latter, what will you do about this?

Should Churches Change?

Arguments against New-Model Churches

I suspect you won't be surprised when I say that the new-model churches aren't without their critics, mostly from those who make up the ranks of established, traditional churches. That's to be expected, as change comes hard for established, tradition-minded people. However, some critics are also within new-paradigm churches, and others are well-known Bible teachers and pastors with a national reputation. Some have come down very hard on the new models and even challenge their orthodoxy. It's imperative that we pay attention to what they're saying, as no one is above error. None of us must be so protective of our churches that we overlook false teaching of any kind. To do so is to violate Scripture. Also there are numerous warnings throughout the Scriptures against teachers who promote and practice false teaching.

My goal in this chapter is twofold. First, I want to address the concept of Christians policing their own ranks. Who is responsible for detecting error in our churches, and how might they accomplish this? Second, what are the arguments being used by those who attempt to police the church ranks for us, especially those who are most suspicious and critical of the new church models? My goal at this point in the book is merely to categorize and present their arguments, not go into any great detail. I simply want you to be aware of what some are saying. Then I'll provide information in chapters 4–8 that will help us address the arguments better and in more detail in chapter 9.

Who Should Address Error?

Churches Must Address Error

The first question is, Who is responsible for addressing error in the church? The answer is the body of Christ. In other words, Christians must police their own. I suspect that most of us see a need for and accept such a practice, yet it makes some very uncomfortable. It goes against their grain. It seems like we're receiving enough criticism from non-Christians, so what's the sense of adding to it? Aren't we merely providing them with more ammunition against us? And isn't there enough conflict in our churches already?

The important question is, What do the Scriptures say about this, and how might we go about it? As we will see below, addressing error in the church is biblical. But I'm not advocating that we form some kind of Christian thought police that assume a "big brother is watching you" approach. George Orwell's book *1984* has come and gone, and we don't need to create a Christian version of it. However, a number of New Testament books address errors that had crept into the early churches, and the obvious implication is that the churches were to deal with them. In the same way, church history is replete with the church taking responsibility to address false teaching, as exemplified by the various church councils.

New Testament Teaching

I could fill this book with examples from the Old Testament of prophets and others who spoke out against error and the practice of error. I could likely do the same with the New Testament. Instead, I will focus your attention on a few key passages that provide the following seven principles that address false teaching. It is clear from the following that the church is responsible not only to identify error but to deal with it.

1. Churches are warned against being led astray by false teaching. Paul writes to the church of the Thessalonians: "Don't let anyone deceive you in any way" (2 Thess. 2:3).

2. Leaders are warned against false teachers. Paul warns Timothy: "If anyone teaches false doctrines and does not agree to the sound instruction of our Lord Jesus Christ and to godly teaching . . ." (1 Tim. 6:3). Peter does much the same in 2 Peter 2:1–3.

3. Leaders have a responsibility to guard or protect biblical doctrine. Paul exhorts Timothy: "Timothy, guard what has been entrusted to your care. Turn away from godless chatter and the opposing ideas of what is falsely called knowledge, which some have professed and in so doing have wandered from the faith" (1 Tim. 6:20–21). Also see 2 Timothy 1:12–14.

4. Leaders are to address or deal with those who teach false doctrine. Paul writes to Timothy: "Command certain men not to teach false doctrines any longer" (1 Tim. 1:3). And he even names some of them, such as Hymenaeus and Philetus (2 Tim. 2:17–18), who taught that the resurrection had already occurred, and Alexander the metalworker who generally opposed Paul's teaching (4:14–15).

5. Leaders are to watch themselves so that they don't teach false doctrine. In 1 Timothy 4:16 Paul writes to Timothy: "Watch your life and doctrine closely. Persevere in them, because if you do, you will save both yourself and your hearers."

6. Leaders are to take great pains to make sure that they handle Scripture accurately and correctly. Paul exhorts Timothy, "Do your best to present yourself to God as one approved, a workman who does not need to be ashamed and who correctly handles the word of truth" (2 Tim. 2:15).

7. Leaders (elders) must firmly hold to sound biblical teaching and use it to encourage the church and refute false teaching (Titus 1:9).

Church Councils

On a number of occasions, churches have come together to address and deal with false teaching. This happened not only in the first century but in later centuries as well. I will briefly mention five occasions that show how the church addressed error.

1. *The Jerusalem Council (AD 49 or 50).* The first council of churches met in Jerusalem, as recorded in Acts 15. Apparently the church at Jerusalem hosted the conference that dealt with the clarity of the gospel. Paul and Barnabas had preached the gospel

to the Gentiles, many of whom had come to faith (vv. 3–4, 7–9). Certain Jews who belonged to the party of the Pharisees were most concerned about this and argued that, for these Gentiles to be saved, they must be circumcised and taught to obey the law of Moses (vv. 1, 5). Ultimately these Jews, Paul, Barnabas, and others traveled to Jerusalem to settle this matter. The final verdict was that salvation is by grace through faith and doesn't involve keeping the law.

2. *The Council of Nicaea (AD 325)*. The next council of churches met in the city of Nicaea. The debate was over the deity of Christ. Arius taught that Jesus Christ was created by God the Father, making him a lesser deity (a view that is held and taught by present-day Jehovah's Witnesses). The final decision of this council affirmed the full deity of the Savior, declaring that he is fully God.

3. *The Council of Constantinople (AD 381)*. This council met in the city of Constantinople. It affirmed the decision at Nicaea regarding Christ's deity. It also affirmed the deity and personality of the Holy Spirit, declaring that he is coequal and coeternal with the Father and Son.

4. *The Council of Ephesus (AD 431)*. This council met in Ephesus to address Nestorius's teaching that emphasized the human nature of Christ. The council proclaimed that Christ had two natures (human and divine) in one divine person.

5. *The Council of Chalcedon (AD 451)*. This council met in the city of Chalcedon. Eutyches was teaching that Christ had only one nature—the divine nature. The Council of Chalcedon affirmed the christological teaching that he had two natures (one divine and one human) in one person with one essence.

The primary biblical-theological concerns of these councils was the clarity of the gospel, Christology or biblical teaching on Christ, and to some degree the Trinity as it relates specifically to Christ and the Holy Spirit. Here we discover that false teaching will always be with us and that it is the responsibility of the church in general and its leaders in particular to address it. The church must be alert to false teaching, and challenge it, explore it, and condemn it.

But that is not enough in itself. The church must also clarify what Scripture teaches. I sense among some in the Emergent Church Movement that they feel a need to go back and reexamine what we believe is the historic, orthodox faith. In response, I believe that we must understand from church history that such reexamination has happened repeatedly throughout the ages as there were many other councils. I don't believe that it hurts for us to reexamine what we believe. Some "buy in" without really thinking carefully about what they're getting. Reexamining the core doctrines of the faith can help us sharpen our thinking and better understand what we believe and why. However, the faith as we now have it has been carefully examined, reexamined, and debated over the last two thousand years. Rest assured that we will not come up with any correction to the historic, orthodox teachings of the faith. If someone does, then I believe that it will be false teaching, and the church is responsible to address and expose it.

How to Address Error

Scripture is very clear that the church in general and leaders in particular are to address error among the people, in a sense, to police the people. For the way to accomplish this, we must turn to Scripture, where we'll find that the answer *is* Scripture. Our core text is 2 Timothy 3:16–17. Here Paul instructs Timothy: "All Scripture is God-breathed and is useful for teaching, rebuking, correcting and training in righteousness, so that the man of God may be thoroughly equipped for every good work."

I want to make several observations on this passage. First, Paul is teaching that the Bible is inspired. Charles Ryrie defines *inspiration* as "God's superintendence of the human authors so that, using their own individual personalities, they composed and recorded without error His revelation to man in the words of the original autographs."[1] Thus the Bible contains God's truth and is the final standard by which we evaluate the church's teaching. Second, note the various uses for the Bible in regard to truth: teaching truth, rebuking those who teach false doctrine, correcting false doctrine, and training people in truth. Third, Paul says that the purpose of all this is to equip the church for good works. Divine truth is critical to what we do in and outside the church. We must know the truth of God's Word to properly apply it.

So how do we practically apply God's Word to address doctrinal error? The church in general and leaders in particular need a biblical-theological grid or sieve that consists of several filters through which they run any and all teaching that claims to be of God. I believe that such a grid is how the church in the first century and the times that followed discerned truth from error. It's not new. In a letter to Martin Luther, Philip Melanchthon, who was considered the theologian of the Reformation, gave us such a biblical-theological grid. It is from this grid that I have developed one that consists of three filters.

Filter 1: The Essentials of the Faith

The first filter consists of the essentials of the faith. These essentials are the propositional truths that are both clearly taught in the Bible and are necessary for one to be considered orthodox. One who is orthodox conforms to the Christian faith as hammered out and represented in the creeds of the early church (see the five councils above). These essentials are the central tenets of the evangelical belief system. Because they are at the core of the gospel, there is no room to flex or wiggle. They draw a doctrinal line in the sand between what is orthodox and unorthodox. Should someone in the church reject any of these views, his or her version of Christianity isn't orthodox. He or she has fallen outside the faith.

There are five essentials: The Bible is the inspired Word of God; there is only one true God as three coequal and coeternal persons (namely, the Trinity); the deity and substitutionary atonement of Christ provide for salvation by faith apart from baptism or works; Christ was bodily resurrected; and Christ will physically return to earth.

The Essentials of the Faith

The inspiration of the Bible as the Word of God

The existence of only one true God as three coequal and coeternal persons (the Trinity)

The deity and substitutionary atonement of Christ

The bodily resurrection of Christ

The physical return of Christ

With those who agree with us on these essentials, we must pursue unity. Paul addresses the church's unity in Ephesians 4:3–16 and commands his church, "Make every effort to keep the unity of the Spirit through the bond of peace" (v. 3). In verse 13 he teaches that this unity in the faith is a sign of the church's spiritual maturity. This is a relational not an organizational unity, based on a common orthodox faith (v. 3; John 17:20–23). Christ commands fellow disciples to love one another (John 13:34–35; 15:12–14). Practically we're willing to relate to one another in various ways: citywide evangelistic crusades, theological societies, and other opportunities.

The essentials, however, are exclusive as well as inclusive. They include people of like mind but exclude people who don't agree on these key points. Examples of the latter are those of a theologically liberal persuasion, Mormons, Jehovah's Witnesses, Unitarians, and all who reject in some way the essentials.

Filter 2: The Nonessentials

The nonessentials are views we hold that may be based on the Scriptures, on tradition, or on both. The nonessentials aren't as clear biblically, and that's why evangelicals disagree on them. However, the reality is that often one group's nonessentials are another group's essentials. Regardless, all are convinced that their view is correct and fully supported by the Bible. Unlike the essentials of the faith, agreement or disagreement on the nonessentials doesn't affect one's orthodoxy, salvation, or standing before Christ. The key word here is *liberty*. There is room to flex.

What are some nonessentials? The following are examples that have proved to be nonessentials but may affect the church's ministries and organization.

1. *Church government (polity).* Polity addresses where the power should be in the church and who makes the major decisions that impact the church. Most churches hold one of three views: the Episcopal form where power is invested in the hands of a bishop outside the local church; the Presbyterian form where power is found in a governing board within the church; the congregational form where the congregation has the power of decision making.
2. *Mode of baptism.* Most who baptize believe in immersion, sprinkling, or pouring.
3. *The Lord's Supper.* The issue is whether the elements convey grace to the recipients. The positions range from an emphatic yes to an equally emphatic no.
4. *The role of women in the church.* The positions range from full participation including ordination and the senior pastor's office to little or no participation at all.
5. *Spiritual gifts.* The positions range from the belief that only some gifts are present today (excluding such gifts as tongues, interpreta-

tion of tongues, prophecy, and healing) to the belief that all the gifts are for today.

6. *When the church meets.* Some argue that it must be on Sunday morning or night, while others argue that any day is permissible. This has been an issue for those churches that are seeker-oriented.

7. *Church practices.* This concerns what the church does when it meets. Some argue, for example, that it must serve communion every time it meets or it must teach the Scriptures. Others feel these aren't necessary every time.

Some Nonessentials of the Faith

Church government (polity)
Mode of baptism
Efficacy of the Lord's Supper
Role of women in the church
Presence and permanence of spiritual gifts
Time and place for the church to meet
Church practices

What should our response be to others regarding the faith nonessentials? We saw that concerning the essentials we are to pursue unity and love. The faith essentials distinguish between those who are within and outside the orthodox faith. We must agree on the essentials or we can't minister together in any way, but we still treat one another with respect as fellow human beings.

Concerning the nonessentials, we are to pursue Christian liberty. Liberty says that it's okay to take a firm position on these issues, but that we're in the realm of interpretive tradition. Though we believe Scripture best supports our view, other intelligent, godly evangelicals hold firmly to differing views for what seem to be good reasons and are still within the orthodox faith.

Christian liberty says we must be willing to grant others these distinctions and still hold one another in high regard. Preserving the "unity of the faith" (Eph. 4:13) means treating others who differ with us on the nonessentials with kindness and compassion (John 13:34–35; 15:12–14, 17). We must not falsely judge or malign them (Rom. 14:9–13). We must also recoil at thinking or claiming that we're the faithful remnant, namely, the only ones with the truth, while all others are wrong and should be condemned. Instead, we choose to treat others as brothers and sisters in Christ. We will revisit this in later chapters as we look at the conduct of some who attack the new-model churches.

I don't believe that I would deny membership in my church to brothers or sisters in Christ who differ over the nonessentials unless their belief was disruptive. However, I might deny them a teaching position or a place on a governing board. Much depends on the particular nonessential and the degree of their fervency.

Filter 3: In All Things Love

The final filter addresses both the essentials and nonessentials. It argues that we must always treat others with love. (In his biblical-theological grid, Melanchthon used the word *charity*.) We are to love those believers who differ on the nonessentials (John 13:34–35; 15:12–14, 17), and, following Christ's example, we are also to love those who differ on the essentials (3:16; Rom. 5:8). This doesn't mean that we are to love what they do or teach, but we are to love them as fellow human beings made in the image of God. We will have to address false teaching and cannot ignore sinful behavior, but we can love the individual while hating his or her sin. This was the Savior's attitude toward lost people ("world") in John 3:16.

I have two gay friends who are my neighbors. Yes, I said "friends." You must understand that I grew up homophobic in a community in the South that didn't tolerate homosexuality. God has helped me to work through my homophobia, and I can say that my wife and I love these two men. However, we neither love nor condone their lifestyle, and they know this. Regardless, God has used our love for them to deeply impact them for the Savior. While many homosexuals are defensive of their lifestyle, one of these men has admitted to me that his lifestyle is wrong. I don't think this would have happened had I rejected or castigated him.

The fact that we are to treat others with love leads next to an important principle or practice that specifically relates to fellow believers. You'll find the principle in Matthew 18:15–20. In verse 15 the Savior teaches, "If your brother sins against you, go and show him his fault, just between the two of you. If he listens to you, you have won your brother over." I see several issues here. First, this would seem to apply primarily to those within the same local church. However, I don't think that anyone would challenge the wisdom of two brothers who belong to different churches getting together to discuss their differences. There seems to be clear precedent for this in Galatians 2:1–10 and the Jerusalem Council in Acts 15.

Second, Jesus commands the offended brother in the Matthew passage to be proactive and approach the offending brother. I suspect this reflects the Savior's practical insight into people. How many times has an offending party come to you over an issue? Likely never.

Third, this is a private meeting. Again this reflects Jesus's wisdom. Whenever we believe someone has wronged us and possibly sinned against us, we are to go to that person before making it public. The reason is obvious—we might be wrong. What if we go public too soon and our information isn't correct? We risk needlessly and sinfully ruining the other's reputation. This has been the fruit of the attacks of some critics on others. In verses 16–18 Jesus continues to address what you should do if the offending party will not listen and address the issue.

An example of how this works is found in Galatians 2:1–16. Peter understood that the gospel had come to the Gentiles, and they could be saved by faith in Christ alone. Thus he as a Jewish believer would fellowship with the Gentile believers. However, when certain men from James came, he disowned the Gentile believers for fear of those who added the requirement of circumcision to the gospel. Since Peter was a pillar and leader in the church, others wrongly followed his example. When Paul saw this, he reproached Peter face-to-face over this issue. It's interesting to note that he did so in front of those Peter had led astray (v. 14). He included the larger group because they were all involved in this sham. By bringing them together, he was able to address the issue with all the participants present.

In summary, a way to capture and express the essence of this grid with its three filters is the following statement based on Melanchthon's teaching: "In essentials, unity; in differences, liberty; in all things, love."

The concepts of the essentials and nonessentials raise several questions for the church concerning application:

- Where do we draw lines and erect fences, if at all?
- Do we let our views on the nonessentials separate us? If so, how much or to what degree?

- Can we do anything together at all? If so, what can we do and to what extent? Can we meet together in fellowship or cooperate on some joint ministry ventures?

Here's another vital question: Are our nonessentials important enough that we want to do any of the following?

- deny someone membership in the church
- exclude a member from speaking or teaching at church
- keep a member off a church board
- challenge or fire a pastor or staff person
- take action that risks dividing or splitting the church
- leave a church
- include nonessentials in a doctrinal statement
- form a new denomination or ministry organization

What the Critics Are Saying

It is safe to say by way of introduction that we would be most naive to believe that some of the following criticisms aren't true of some of those who are developing new-model churches. However, it is equally naive to believe, as many critics imply, that the criticisms are all true of all of the new models. Not only is it naive, but this sort of claim runs into a logical problem or thinking error known as the sweeping generalization—where we sweep everyone under the same carpet!

Those who are detractors and critics of the new church models mount a number of arguments against them and the changes they've brought to how we do church. I collected most from personal letters, one-on-one conversations, anti-seeker websites, and some books and articles. As I studied them, I found that many are similar and fall under certain categories. I organized them into six categories and present them below with some explanation to help clarify the position. I will not, however, respond here to the arguments. I address them in general in the chapters that follow and more specifically in chapter 9, where I'll give the pros and cons of each.

1. *The proclamation of Scripture.* This first category addresses the general teaching and preaching of God's Word. Critics argue that the

new models in general and the seeker church in particular minimize and downplay the proclamation of God's Word. For example, they say the preaching is topical, not expositional. Also the sermons are more "feel good," practical messages, a soft sell of Christianity.

2. *The focus of Sunday morning worship.* The second category addresses what new-paradigm churches do in their services on Sunday mornings. The critics argue that Sunday morning services in these churches focus incorrectly on the unsaved rather than the saved. Sunday morning should be a time of edification for the church, not evangelism for the lost. What they mean is that corporate worship that usually or normally takes place on Sunday mornings is for believers, not unbelievers. They say that Sunday morning worship in the new models is high-tech, slick entertainment that caters to the crowds, not the committed people of God.

3. *The church and evangelism.* This criticism is based on the church's purpose for evangelism and the message of the gospel. Critics argue that the new-paradigm churches soft-pedal the gospel to keep people in the pews. They do preach a gospel message, but it is so compromised that it fails in its primary purpose to move people out of the fallen world and into the kingdom of God.

4. *The church's means or methodology for ministry.* The focus here is on how the new churches are doing ministry. Some would say this addresses their philosophy of ministry. The critics argue that the church must not use secular means, such as marketing, in its attempts to reach people both saved and lost. The church is taking its cues from the world, using entertainment and marketing devices, such as film clips, skits, comedy, pyrotechnics, light shows, and overindulgence in music. An example would be the seeker church methodology that claims to take a poll of lost people, find out what they want in religion, and then make an all-out effort in the church to provide what they want.

5. *The motives for the church's ministry.* The critics challenge the motivation of the new-model churches for doing what they do. Much of what the new churches are doing is drawing in numbers to fill the pews. They soft-pedal the gospel to keep people in the pews. They seek to appeal to the desires of the unregenerate person—a direct appeal to the flesh.

6. *The church's goal for ministry in general.* The new-model church's goal is to bring in lots of people, keep them interested in the church, and get them to come back next week.

Questions for Reflection and Discussion

1. Do you believe that churches in general and leaders in particular have the responsibility to protect their congregations from false teaching? Why or why not? Who is responsible for this in your church? Is this stated anywhere, such as in your constitution, bylaws, policies, and so on?
2. Do you believe that churches in general and leaders in particular are responsible to protect other congregations from false teaching? Why or why not?
3. How does your church and its leaders protect people from false teaching? What safeguards are in place to make sure that your teaching is sound?
4. Does your church hold to the essentials of the faith? How do you know? What are they? How often are they covered in some way during an average church year?
5. Identify your church's nonessentials. Do you treat them as essentials or nonessentials? Do you have a church doctrinal statement? Are any of your nonessentials included in that statement?
6. How would your church's nonessentials affect someone's membership in the church? Would someone with different opinions be excluded from speaking or teaching in church? Why or why not?
7. Would your church hire a pastor who disagrees with any or all of your nonessentials?
8. If a member disagreed with any or all of your nonessentials, would you allow this person to be on your church board?
9. Are you aware of any critics' arguments against the new-model churches? Where did you hear about them? What are they? Are there any people in your congregation who are critics of the new-model churches?
10. Are you a critic of new-model churches? Why or why not? If so, are you willing to give this book a fair hearing?

Part 2

Changing Churches

Doing Church

Interpreting the Biblical Passages

The Scriptures are the basis for our faith and practice. My experience is that regardless of where one stands on the new-model churches, all agree that we must know and follow what the Bible teaches about how we do church. The obvious question is, What does the Bible teach? The problem for those pursuing new ways and forms of doing church is answering the question unanimously. But I would argue that an equally important question that must be answered first is, How do we interpret the passages that address in some way what the Bible teaches about doing church? At the root of our understanding of the Scriptures is how we interpret the Scriptures. (This is popularly known in Bible studies and seminary circles as hermeneutics.)

Some have pointed out that you can make the Bible say anything you want, and they are correct. I believe that a major reason for the different views of the new paradigm leaders and their critics is based on how they handle, mishandle, or don't handle Scripture that addresses church ministry.

I have divided this chapter into two parts. The first presents the problem—that various people view church ministry differently. The second proposes a solution—a solid, biblical hermeneutic for handling the passages that address church ministry. As we discover and discuss the biblical passages on doing church, my desire is that we arrive at a solid hermeneutic for doing church.[1]

The Problem of Different Views of Church Ministry

The different views that various churches, church leaders, and denominations have regarding how churches should conduct their ministries are based on different interpretations of the Bible. This raises several important questions. Why are there so many different interpretations? Why can't all the churches agree on what the Bible says about ministry and simply get on with the task?

There are at least two reasons for the different views of ministry. One is the influence of tradition in the church, and the other is the hermeneutic or lack of one embraced by the church.

The Influence of Tradition

One reason so many interpret the Bible differently stems from widely divergent church traditions. I define church tradition as the nonbiblical ideas and practices that church people attempt to practice, preserve, and pass on to the next generation. When I use the term *nonbiblical*, I'm not using it in a negative sense. I simply mean that you won't find these ideas in the Bible, not that they contradict the Bible. Some examples are Wednesday night prayer meetings, singing the great hymns of the faith, the Sunday school program, the way a church takes the offering, the importance of pastoral visitation, and church potlucks. These are nonbiblical practices, because Scripture doesn't clearly mandate them and in some cases doesn't even mention them. And the church comes to observe and value them to the extent that they become an integral part of the church's culture. The natural inclination is to pass them on to the next generation. As one old-timer put it, "If they're good enough for us, they ought to be good enough for our kids and grandkids!"

As long as a church exists, it will embrace tradition. It is simply a part of who we are. And our traditions—both good and bad—exert a profound influence on how we and our churches view and interpret the Scriptures. People read the Bible through the lens of their church traditions. And there are two kinds of traditions—those that are supposedly based on the Bible and those not based on the Bible.

Traditions Based on the Bible

Traditions that are supposedly based on the Bible are those that many congregants believe are the clear teaching of God's Word. It is a dangerous situation when we don't recognize these practices as tradition and, instead, believe they are biblical mandates demanding our allegiance. So how can we distinguish between these traditions and the clear teaching of the Bible? The answer is to determine the essentials and nonessentials of the faith. As we discovered in chapter 3, the essentials of the faith are those propositional truths that are taught in the Bible and are necessary to believe if one is to be considered orthodox (conforming to the faith of the early church as recognized over the years and presented in the church's creeds). They include such doctrines as the inspiration of the Bible and the Trinity.

The nonessentials of the faith are views that we hold to be based on Scripture, tradition, or both. They are not clearly biblical, so Christians have disagreed over them throughout history and still disagree today. They include such beliefs as church government (congregational, Presbyterian, or Episcopal), the proper mode of baptism, the role of women in the church, the presence and permanency of certain spiritual gifts, and others. Here's the test: If the majority of orthodox believers place what you believe under the faith nonessentials, then you are most likely dealing with church tradition that is supposedly based on the Bible but may not be. Thus you would be wise not to insist that your church embrace these beliefs as faith essentials. An example would be the mode of baptism. While a church may believe that it is proper to immerse, many orthodox churches throughout history have differed and practiced other forms. The church may practice immersion but should be willing to adopt another form if an individual requests it or his or her situation merits it.

Traditions Clearly Not Based on the Bible

Some church traditions make no claim to be based on Scripture. There is no flipping to various texts in the Bible when congregants discuss them. The problem is that many in our churches wrongly assume—whether consciously or unconsciously—that these practices are based squarely on Scripture or were practiced by all the New Testament churches. Their assumption is "We've always done it this way. Therefore it must be based on the Bible!"

Some examples are the church's liturgy, pews, kneelers, an altar, stained glass windows, collection plates, clerical robes and collars, and the architectural style of the church's building. While such traditions may not be harmful to the life of the church, they could be. There are good and bad church traditions. What is the difference? Good church tradition is always subservient to the Bible.

Good Tradition

Tradition does not equal Scripture.
Scripture is above tradition.

Bad traditions are the church's traditions that, knowingly or unknowingly, it equates with the Bible's teaching or even holds above Scripture.

Bad Tradition

Tradition equals Scripture.
Tradition is above Scripture.

An example from Scripture is found in Mark 7:1–13, where the Pharisees criticized Jesus's disciples for not following their tradition of ceremonially washing their hands before eating. The Pharisees were in the habit of setting aside the biblical imperative to honor one's father and mother by withholding help from them because that help was supposedly devoted to God. Jesus makes a clear distinction between Scripture and tradition (in this case bad tradition) when he says of them, "You have let go of the commands of God and are holding on to the traditions of men" (v. 8).

A contemporary example is the prevalent view that a congregation hires the pastor to do the work of its ministry. Paul is very clear in Ephesians 4:7–13 that the church is to be involved in accomplishing its ministry, and certain gifted individuals, such as pastors, are to equip them for this. The real problem for the church is that those who embrace good or bad tradition often insist that the traditions are binding on all Christians because "we've always done it that way," or "that's the way we do things around here," or because we're simply afraid of change.

The Church's Need for a Hermeneutic

The fact that the church has traditions—both good and bad—is one reason for all the different interpretations of how the church should conduct its ministries. The church needs a clear biblical hermeneutic for interpreting the biblical teaching on ministry. Since hermeneutics addresses how to interpret the Bible, I am arguing that we need a proper biblical hermeneutic to interpret not only the Bible in general but the passages that address the church's ministry in particular.

Most people who attend and/or minister in churches have some kind of hermeneutic for interpreting the Scriptures. Most often it is the same literal approach they use when reading the newspaper or a good novel. And this is a good approach; however, reading the book of Acts, which says much about church ministry, and reading the morning paper involve differing levels of complexity. Some of the errors that I've observed come from reading one's beliefs into the Bible; that is, people impose their views on doing church on the text rather than letting the text speak to them. For example, if we assume that women can be senior pastors of churches, we may read and interpret passages on women and ministry accordingly.

Another error is taking passages out of their context. I had one critic of the new-model churches explain to me that he approached the Scriptures like the Bereans in Acts 17:11 who "examined the Scriptures every day to see if what Paul said was true." He was most surprised when I asked if he was a Christian and then pointed out that the Bereans were unbelieving Jews. He had simply missed this in the context of the passage (see verses 10 and 12 in particular). While not much harm was done in this situation, it is a reminder that it is imperative, when interpreting a passage of Scripture, that we take into consideration its context. Most, if not all, bad theology is the result of interpreting passages out of their proper context.

The people in our churches need not only a general knowledge of how to interpret the Bible but also an understanding of how to interpret the biblical passages that address ministry in the local church. The Bible doesn't say as much about this topic as some might think. I believe it was because the Godhead desires that the church have much freedom in how it conducts ministry. However, the book of Acts (the church history book of the New Testament) gives us information on this topic, as do some of Paul's epistles. The key hermeneutical question is, How do we interpret the texts we do have on the first-century church? And even more to the issue, Must congregations today emulate the practices of the early church? Unfortunately, few today have addressed this issue with any depth.

A Special Hermeneutic for Church Ministry

As we have seen, there is disagreement about how the church should conduct its ministries. The only way churches can agree on what the Bible says and then get on with the task is to arrive at a proper biblical hermeneutic for church ministry. In the rest of this chapter I provide such a hermeneutic that presents three approaches or principles that cover what the Bible teaches about the church and its ministries. These are normative principles that apply to all people everywhere at all times.[2]

The Descriptive versus the Prescriptive Principle

A major question facing contemporary church leaders is whether certain first-century practices are normative for churches today simply because they appear in the Bible. For example, if Luke in Acts describes some aspect of a church's ministry, should today's churches not only learn from but replicate that ministry?

The Descriptive Principle

Most who follow a descriptive approach to Scripture would answer yes to the above question. And there was a time early in my church ministry when I would have agreed, for three reasons: First, since these descriptive passages appear in the Bible, they must be biblical. And because they're biblical, we must comply with them. Second, the Bible is our sole guide for both faith and practice. If we follow the Bible for our doctrine, we should do the same for our practices, and this includes the church's ministries. Third, the early church set a historical precedent for all future congregations. We would be wise to follow that precedent.

A subtle assumption undergirds the thinking of most of these arguments—that all the New Testament churches basically functioned the same way. Therefore, if we discover what one did, we can know what all of them practiced. Or we can take the various bits of information scattered throughout the New Testament that describe what the early churches practiced, put them together like the pieces of a puzzle, and get a single picture of the early church that represents a common model or pattern depicting what they all must have done.

The descriptive principle is flawed, however, for several reasons. First, simply because the New Testament describes a church practice doesn't make it mandatory. For example, the Jerusalem church met in homes and in the temple courts (Acts 2:46; 3:11). The descriptive principle, if it's to be consistent, would argue that churches today must meet in homes or in something similar to a temple court. I'm not aware of any critic of new-model churches who would promote this interpretation.

Second, mandatory practices are prescribed in the Bible. For example, the Lord and later Paul in 1 Corinthians 11:23–26 clearly command that the church is to celebrate the Lord's Supper. "Do this in remembrance of me" (v. 24). Thus all churches everywhere at all times must comply.

Third, descriptive passages describe what took place in one particular church, but not necessarily in other churches, and certainly not all churches in the New Testament era. For example, the church at Troas may have met regularly on the first day of the week to break bread (Acts 20:7), but there's no evidence that other churches or *all* churches followed suit.

Fourth, there must be evidence in these descriptive passages that the author was establishing a precedent. For example, in Acts 20:7–12 Luke may be describing what was a meeting of the local church, though we can't be sure of this. Regardless, some use this passage to argue that because Paul preached at night, the legitimate meeting of the church should take place at night. In response, we must ask, Was Luke's intent here to establish a fixed meeting time for all churches everywhere? Is that the primary reason for his including this story in the text? According to Acts 1:8, I believe that his primary purpose was to show how the Lord was powerfully at work in spreading his gospel through witnesses like Paul, not dictating when all churches at all times are to meet.

The Prescriptive Principle

Prescriptive, not descriptive, passages are divine precepts that address and mandate how churches are to conduct their ministries. Some examples follow:

1. It's imperative that the church make disciples (Matt. 28:19–20).
2. The church must meet together regularly (Heb. 10:25).
3. The church must observe the ordinances of the Lord's Supper and baptism (Matt. 26:26–29; 28:19; Acts 2:38; 1 Cor. 11:23–26).
4. The church must teach the Bible (2 Tim. 4:2).
5. The church must obey its leaders (Heb. 13:17).

How might we spot prescriptive passages? Usually they contain commands or imperatives, and you don't need to know Greek to spot them. A good English translation will do. For example, in Matthew 28:19 Jesus commands his followers: "Make disciples." In Hebrews 10:25 the writer commands his readers: "Let us not give up meeting together." In 1 Corinthians 11:24 Jesus is quoted as saying, "Do this [Lord's Supper] in remembrance of me." In 2 Timothy 4:2 Paul commands, "Preach the Word." In Hebrews 13:17 the writer exhorts his listeners, "Obey your leaders and submit to their authority."

The Negative versus the Positive Principle

Contemporary church leaders must also consider whether church practices can be legitimate if they are not found in the Bible.

The Negative Principle

The negative principle argues that if a practice isn't found in the Bible, we can't do it. Some have used the following motto to state this position: "Where the Bible speaks, we speak; and where the Bible is silent, we're silent."

The core of this issue is one of presence or absence. If you can find a certain church practice in the Bible, it's biblical and permissible. If you can't, it's not biblical and is forbidden. For example, some would argue that it is wrong for churches to use musical instruments in their worship services because, supposedly, you can't find any example of this in the Bible. Some would question the practice of hiring one pastor to lead a church, asking, Where is there an example of this practice in the Bible? Church membership is another practice that is questioned, because there are no examples of church membership in the Bible. Other common practices that are not mentioned in the Bible are congregational voting and membership in a denomination.

There are several reasons, however, why this principle isn't correct. Here are three. First, the argument simply doesn't make sense. For example, I live in Dallas, Texas. The legal codes of Dallas say nothing about permission to cook hot dogs or hamburgers on the grill in my backyard. Therefore, according to the negative principle, I cannot and should not cook these items in my backyard. That doesn't make sense, does it?

Second, just because a certain church practice isn't found in the Scriptures doesn't mean the church didn't do it. This is an argument from silence that is a very poor argument to begin with. Absence of proof isn't proof of absence. Common sense tells us that some, if not most, of the practices of the New Testament churches aren't mentioned in Scripture. When a practice isn't mentioned in the New Testament, it doesn't necessarily mean that the early church didn't do it. I suspect that there were many things they did that aren't mentioned due to their lack of importance. Also such mention would make some books, such as Acts, very long accounts. In addition, the fact that the church didn't use a practice doesn't mean that it was wrong. They may not have followed a certain ministry practice because they lacked the funds or the time.

Third, no one can consistently apply the negative hermeneutic. The proponents of the negative principle have certain practices that aren't found in the Scriptures. For example, they use hymnals from which they sing the great hymns of the faith, many have a preaching service on Sunday mornings at 11:00 a.m., they conduct Sunday school or similar classes, they meet on Wednesday nights for prayer, they provide nursery care for people's infants, they speak with the aid of microphones, they communicate using email, and so on. So if you follow the negative principle, where and how do you draw the line?

The Positive Principle

The positive principle argues that the church is free to pursue practices that aren't found in the Bible, as long as they are not prohibited by the clear teaching of Scripture. God's Word is the final authority in these matters. God is a God of grace who gives his church freedom to be creative and pursue new ways of doing ministry. This is not only true of such practices as instrumental worship, congregational voting, a Sunday school program, and many others, but it is true of other forms of ministry. An example is the use of technology. Today's technology was unknown to the church of the first century. Ministry over the Internet and video presentations during sermons weren't possible then. Rather than banning such practices from the church because they aren't found in the Bible or because we've never done it that way before, the church has the freedom to use them in ways that promote the gospel.

There is some inconsistency in this view as well. Some believe that using older, often outdated forms of technology, such as microphones, telephones, electric typewriters, and so on, is okay, but they refuse to use newer, updated forms of technology, such as the computer, email, and so on. Again, where does one draw the line?

The Pattern versus the Principle Approach

Another question for the contemporary church to ponder is whether we must follow the practices of the early church or just the principles behind these practices.

The Pattern Approach

Generally proponents of the pattern approach argue that the practices or patterns of the apostles and the early church are universal and binding on all congregations everywhere at all times. God saw fit to record in the Bible the patterns of the early church as a blueprint or guide to help all Christians in the following centuries to know how best to conduct their ministries. In other words, today's churches must do ministry the way yesterday's church did ministry.

Supporters provide at least three arguments for this approach. First, Christ and his apostles established the New Testament church—its structure, forms, and ministries. Who are we to question what they've done? It's presumptuous on our part to think that we could do it better than they. Hence, it's imperative that we follow what they've set in place. Second, God blessed the early church and its ministries the way they did ministry. Thus if we do ministry the way they did ministry, he'll likely bless us too. Third, Scripture teaches that congregations today must observe the biblical practices and patterns of the New Testament church. According to passages such as 1 Corinthians 11:16 and 14:33–37, God, through Paul, has enjoined today's churches to follow certain practices of yesterday's churches. In short, apostolic precept is apostolic practice. Along with these, supporters embrace also some of the arguments used by those who have adopted the descriptive and negative principles.

When churches follow the pattern approach, there are several practices that must be part of their ministries. For example, the church must be led not by one person, such as a senior pastor, but by a plurality of leaders called elders. The New Testament teaches that elders are the leaders of each church—Acts 14:23; 15:2; 20:17; 1 Timothy 5:17; James 5:14; and 1 Peter 5:2. Another is that the primary meeting of the first-century church took place at night, according to Acts 20:7–12. While it's okay for a church to meet during the day, the primary meeting of today's churches must be at night. Therefore, the church must maintain—not abandon—a Sunday evening meeting. A third practice is that every time the church met, it observed the Lord's Supper as a key worship function, according to 1 Corinthians 11:17–34. Thus today's churches should observe the Lord's Supper weekly. My point is that, according to those who hold to patternism, these practices as well as others aren't optional. If you don't practice these, you aren't biblical and are in violation of the New Testament teaching for the church. You may also find yourself greatly criticized by the advocates of patternism.

There are a number of reasons why this approach to interpreting the verses on doing church isn't correct. Patternism assumes wrongly that all the early churches shared the same practices and patterns—that they all were alike. In reality they were made up of culturally distinct congregations, and there is biblical evidence for this. In one case other churches did follow the lead of one church—Corinth—in the role of women in worship (1 Cor. 11:16). However, in many situations they didn't. For example, the Jerusalem church met daily (Acts 2:46), whereas the church at Troas met on the first day of the week (20:7). Paul advised the widows in Ephesus to remarry (1 Tim. 5:14) but those in Corinth to remain single (1 Cor. 7:39–40). The Jerusalem Council urged Gentile converts to "abstain from food sacrificed to idols" (Acts 15:29), but Paul permitted the practice in Corinth (1 Corinthians 8–10). And we must take note that Paul specifically applied the local imperative in 1 Corinthians 14:33–37 to the Corinthian church ("I am writing to you"—v. 37), not all churches at all times.

The passages cited for a plurality of elders in every church fail to take into account the city church–house church model of the New Testament churches. For example, in Acts 20:17 Paul sent for the elders of the church at Ephesus. This was the city church. These elders were the pastors of the various house churches in Ephesus that made up the city church (v. 20) of Ephesus.[3] There is also biblical evidence that James was the lead pastor of the church at Jerusalem (Acts 12:17; 15; 21:18; Gal. 2:9, 12).

The following is a summary of the shortcomings of patternism.

- Patternism wrongly presumes that all first-century churches shared the same practices and patterns.
- If all congregations are to follow early church practices, then which early church do we follow—the church at Rome, Ephesus, Corinth, and so on?
- We have very little information on the practices of the early or apostolic churches. How would we fill in the gaps to have a complete picture?

- To be consistent, we must follow all, not just some, of the early churches' practices and patterns.
- Just because the apostolic churches followed certain practices, it doesn't mean that all churches everywhere must do the same.
- We must determine if an author's intent for including a particular apostolic church practice in the biblical account was to establish a precedent for all churches everywhere.
- Many of the early church practices are descriptive in nature and were not binding on the church at any time.
- Patternism poses the potential for condemnation of those who disagree, a judgmental attitude, and pride.
- The church is dynamic in nature and has changed sufficiently so that apostolic practices don't fit today's nonapostolic church.

The Principle Approach

The principle approach argues that the church is obligated to follow only the principles, not necessarily the patterns and practices, of the early church. This view is based on the premise that the principles of Scripture are normative for all churches everywhere. They are stated as clear propositions of Scripture. Those who support patternism would agree with these principles. If we were to collect all of them, we would have a theology of the church or what theologians call an ecclesiology. The following are some examples of these clear propositions that are binding on all churches everywhere.

- The church's beliefs are based on Scripture (2 Tim. 3:16–17).
- The church's purpose is to glorify God (Rom. 15:5–6; 1 Cor. 6:20; 10:31).
- The church's mission is to make disciples (Matt. 28:19–20; Mark 16:15).
- The church is the body of Christ universal and local (Matt. 16:16–19; Acts 9:31; Eph. 1:22–23; Col. 1:18, 24).
- The church is to meet together regularly (Heb. 10:25).
- The church is to celebrate the ordinances (Matt. 26:26–29; 28:19; Acts 2:38; 1 Cor. 11:23–26).
- The church is to discipline its people (Matt. 18:15–17; 1 Cor. 5:1–5).
- The church is to teach the Bible (2 Tim. 4:2).

- The church is to evangelize the lost (Matt. 28:19–20; Col. 4:3–6).
- The church is to obey its leaders (Heb. 13:17).
- The church is to pay its workers (1 Cor. 9:14; 1 Tim. 5:17–18).

Questions for Reflection and Discussion

1. Do you agree or disagree with the author's position on the pre-scriptive, positive, and principle approaches to the handling of passages on church ministries? Why or why not? If not, how would you respond to his arguments?
2. Like the author, have you unknowingly bought into the descriptive, negative, or pattern approaches in the past? Which one? How did this affect your ministry?
3. What are some of your church's ministry practices that you can't find in the Bible? Do they differ with or contradict the clear teaching of Scripture? Is it okay to permit these practices? Why or why not?
4. It is natural for churches to want to follow early church practices. What first-century practices does your church follow? Why? Is this okay? Shouldn't other churches follow them as well? Explain.
5. If you agree with the author's position, how will you handle those who differ with you and criticize your handling of Scripture on church ministries? Are there people in your church currently who are doing this? How have you dealt with them?

The Changing Church

Developing a Theology of Change

How many times have you heard an old-timer say, "The only things you can be sure of these days are death and taxes"? I think that's wrong. The only things you can be sure of are death, taxes, and change. Change has become a constant in the twenty-first century, and it affects the church as well as the rest of society. Presently, far too many churches are unsure about accepting change, which is no way to approach ministry and the various church models in the early twenty-first century. A church's view of change will have a major impact on its ability to minister. Those that remain resistant to change will likely not survive.

Not only is change a constant, it's a constant whirling vortex that can swallow up churches as well as other organizations that don't know how to deal with it. I believe that a major reason why 80 to 85 percent of the churches in North America are plateaued or in decline is because they don't know how to deal with spiraling, turbulent change. Many are afraid of change, and their response to it is to become passive. Someone in the church—often the board but sometimes the pastor—bugles a retreat and everyone falls back. Others get angry over change. They see their cherished traditions dying, they don't like it, and they may lash out at those who suggest that the church needs to minister in new ways.

More change took place in the latter half of the twentieth century than has occurred since the founding of this nation. Currently we are experiencing a major transformation that is rearranging society as we've known it—its worldview, basic values, social and political structures, arts, and key institutions. A whole new world—the postmodern world—is emerging that is different from the world in which many in our churches grew up.

We must not assume, however, that churches in the first century and throughout history didn't have to deal with change. Read the book of Acts and church history and you'll discover that is not the case. Thus I contend that the church has always needed a theology of change, and this need will only increase in the future. The tragedy is that, unlike churches of the first century, few churches today have addressed the issue. Far too many have retreated into their fortresses and pulled up their drawbridges in an attempt to avoid change altogether. A better approach is to work to understand change, learn to live with it, and develop ways to use it to their advantage in ministry. Key to this happening is the development of a theology of change.

We must be active and aggressive when it comes to handling change in our churches. After all, change is what Christianity is all about—the transformation of one's life to Christlikeness (2 Cor. 3:18). However, it is most difficult to be active and aggressive unless you have a theology of change that's true to the Bible and will guide you through the change process. Every Christian institution—whether it's a church or parachurch ministry—has to wrestle with the vexing question, What must and must not change? To answer this question for our churches, those of us who will lead them in the twenty-first century must have a theology of change. A good theology of change consists of the three Fs: *function*, *form*, and *freedom*, and the rest of this chapter will address them.

Function

Let's begin with the first F—the concept of *function*. First, we need a definition of *function*, then I'll provide several examples and explore how to discover the functions of a church.

The Definition of a Function

I define the functions of the church as the timeless, unchanging, and nonnegotiable precepts that are based on Scripture and are mandates for all churches to pursue to accomplish their purpose.

But what does this mean? In this definition there are six characteristics of a church's functions that make them absolutes.

Timeless

Functions are timeless. As long as there is a church, they must be present. They were true of Christ's church in the first century, they'll continue to be true of his church in the twenty-first century, and they'll be true as long as the church remains on earth. For example, evangelism—as a function—characterized the first-century church, and it should characterize twenty-first-century churches as well. This must never change.

Unchanging

Functions are unchanging. God didn't make evangelism or worship functions of the first-century church, and then change them for the twentieth- or twenty-first-century church. Christ instituted certain functions for his church at Pentecost that will remain the same until he takes his church home. Consequently, it doesn't matter how much change sweeps across the church. It must not abandon these functions. They're here to stay.

Nonnegotiable

Functions are nonnegotiable. As churches of the first century couldn't pick and choose the functions they would observe or ignore, neither can the church in the twenty-first century if it wants to be an obedient church. A number of churches in North America are "niche churches." These are churches that are known for a particular ministry strength. For instance, in several of the larger cities in the Bible Belt, some churches are strong in the area of family ministries and children's programs. Another is strong in counseling. Others are strong in preaching and teaching the Bible or worship. Though churches will have certain strengths,

> Functions are the timeless, unchanging, and nonnegotiable precepts that are based on Scripture and are mandates for all churches to pursue to accomplish their purpose.

Christ has commanded all churches to "make disciples" (Matt. 28:19–20), not to "make niches." A church's success is based on its disciples, not its niches. So are these churches wrong? I believe they are, and my beef is that in so many of them evangelism is extremely weak or nonexistent. They've unconsciously negotiated evangelism away for some other function, such as worship or teaching, and that contradicts Christ's Great Commission and negatively affects the church long term.

Based on the Bible

Functions are based on the Bible. We find the functions in the Bible; therefore, they must be biblical. In 2 Timothy 3:16–17 Paul writes: "All Scripture is God-breathed and is useful for teaching, rebuking, correcting and training in righteousness, so that the man of God may be thoroughly equipped for every good work." We may find the functions in such biblical passages as Acts 2:42–47 (biblical teaching, fellowship, worship, service, evangelism, and so on). However, as we learned in chapter 4, for them to be functions, they must be prescriptive. A number of passages affirm that the functions in Acts 2:42–47 are prescriptive as well (1 Cor. 11:23–26; Col. 4:2; 1 Tim. 4:13; and others).

Mandates for the Church

These timeless functions serve as mandates for the church. Since they are timeless, unchanging, and based on the Bible, they comprise the local church's ministry precepts. If you want to know what your church should be doing and what you have in common with the churches of the first century, discover the church's functions. Consequently, they are absolutes that are to be a part of every church's ministry. The implication is that all churches must pursue all the functions and not just those that fit into their particular ministry niche. If a church is weak in evangelism and strong in Bible teaching, it needs to work hard at becoming stronger in its evangelistic efforts. If it is weak in good Bible teaching but strong in worship or evangelism, it needs to work hard to develop its Bible teaching. I would challenge churches to make a list of their functions and then evaluate how they're doing. In addition, the functions are for all believers in the church and not just a few, because they are necessary for one to develop into a spiritually mature Christian.

Serve a Purpose

Finally, the church's functions serve a purpose. Functions such as fellowship, evangelism, and worship all work together to accomplish the church's overall purpose—to glorify God (Rom. 15:6; 1 Cor. 6:20; 10:31). But what does it mean to glorify God? So many use this term and don't take time to define it. In the Old Testament the term (*kabod*—"to be heavy") has the idea of reputation or honor. In the New Testament it is used of honor in the sense of recognition or acclaim (Luke 14:10; Rev. 14:7). Thus, bringing these concepts together, we generally glorify God when we uphold his reputation so that he receives recognition and honor. This should take place both within and outside the church, the latter involving in particular the unbelieving communities where churches are located.

Characteristics of Functions

Timeless

Unchanging

Nonnegotiable

Based on the Bible

Mandates

Serve a purpose

The Church's Functions

I divide the church's functions into two categories—general and specific. The church's general functions are those for which all believers are responsible. They apply to all believers at all times and are vital to their spiritual maturity. Specific functions are those that apply only to certain believers, not all believers, and aren't necessary to spiritual maturity. Examples are leadership, administration, and others. Some congregants are leaders while others are followers. I want to focus here on the church's general functions.

I believe that there are five general church functions. They are teaching, fellowship, worship, evangelism, and service. All are found in Acts 2:42–47 and are prescribed in other parts of the New Testament. All five of them must be somewhat balanced and are necessary in a church's ministry if its people are to become spiritually mature.

Teaching

One vital function of the church is teaching or instruction. According to Luke, the Jerusalem church "devoted themselves to the apostles' teaching" (Acts 2:42). Just as Jesus had taught his disciples, they were to teach others. You'll find both the verb *to teach* and the noun *teaching* used approximately 130 times in the New Testament. Apollos provides us with an example of one who taught Scripture (18:24–28), as well as Paul, Timothy, Titus, and many others. Paul seems to have been a master teacher who taught Timothy and Titus, who in turn taught others. For example, he instructs Timothy, "Watch your life and doctrine closely" (1 Tim. 4:16). He instructs Titus, "You must teach what is in accord with sound doctrine" (Titus 2:1). In fact, the pastoral epistles contain close to fifty references to some form of teaching. Paul also teaches Timothy that the local church is to be the "foundation of the truth" (1 Tim. 3:15). The idea is that the local church is to be the place where truth can be found. And truth is found, of course, in Scripture. In 2 Timothy 3:16 Paul tells Timothy, "All Scripture is God-breathed and is useful for teaching," as well as other things.

I must emphasize the importance of the application of taught truth to the Christian's life. I have a saying: "If you cut me, I bleed Bible Church." What that means is that for much of my life as a believer I've been influenced by the Teaching Church or Bible Church Movement. These are churches that are very strong in teaching Scripture. However, the older, more traditional Bible Churches emphasized primarily the teaching of Scripture over the other four functions. Also they taught that a knowledge of Scripture was the primary door to spiritual maturity. People who know the Bible well are mature Christians.

My experience has shown, though, that while some of these people are mature, many aren't. In the 1980s and 1990s in Dallas, when the pastoral staffs of some of these churches attempted to lead them to a more contemporary approach to ministry, I observed that these people could be just as nasty and mean as those who don't know the Bible well. Not only must congregants know the Bible well, they must apply or live the Bible well. This calls for obedience to the taught word. In Matthew 28:20 Jesus speaks of "teaching them to obey everything I have commanded you." Thus teaching all nations to obey everything he commanded is vital to making disciples. Spiritual maturity involves both a knowledge of the Bible and its application to one's life.

At this point you might want to call into question my prescriptive use of a descriptive text (Acts 2:42 is descriptive). You have read the previous chapter where I argue against this very practice and you are thinking, *This guy's a hypocrite. He's doing the very thing he warned us against in the last chapter!* I do this here because there are numerous passages (some of which I quoted above) that prescribe or enjoin the teaching of God's Word. And the same is true of the other functions. We must not treat descriptive passages prescriptively. However, there may be other texts that prescribe functions that are found in descriptive passages. Such is the case with Acts 2:42–47. Then it's okay.

Fellowship

A second vital function of the church is fellowship. Luke writes of the early church, "They devoted themselves to the apostles' teaching and to the fellowship" (Acts 2:42). The writer of Hebrews commands, "Let us not give up meeting together, as some are in the habit of doing" (Heb. 10:25).

I suspect that the average churched person thinks of standing around and drinking coffee and eating donuts when he or she hears the word *fellowship*. The Greek word Luke used for fellowship is *koinonia*. It appears only here in the book of Acts and not at all in Luke's Gospel. Its meaning is "a close relationship, an association, fellowship, and communion." The believers experienced some type of close relationship or association with one another. Today the term *community* has become popular among younger believers and has probably the same or a similar meaning as *fellowship*.

So fellowship is much more than coffee and donuts before Sunday school class. That doesn't go deep enough. *Fellowship* signifies a strong human relationship or, better, a deep friendship that is reflected in the use of the word *together* as experienced by the Jerusalem church in Acts 2:44 and 46. It involves doing life deeply together. And I believe that it is best summed up in the sixty-four "one another" passages sprinkled throughout the New Testament. More than half of these passages instruct believers to love one another (see John 13:34 and 1 John 3:23 as examples).

Believers and unbelievers alike—especially younger ones—yearn for this kind of relationship and look for it within the church. And if they don't find it there, they look for it in other places outside the church, such as the workplace, sports, clubs, and bars. Churches that desire to reach people and minister to them, especially younger believers, need to develop ministries that address this deeply felt need for fellowship. One form or practice that has become very popular and addresses this need is a small-group ministry. In fact, small-group ministries are beginning to replace the large-group worship-preaching session as the primary way younger people assimilate into today's churches.

Some churches emphasize fellowship to the exclusion of the other four functions. These are what I refer to as family or nursing home churches, where people not only value time together but expect the pastor, whom they view as a chaplain, to take care of them and meet their needs. Unfortunately, their brand of fellowship is surface only, and many of them, the men in particular (mostly the Builder generation), value friendship as long as no one gets too close. Contrary to Christ's direction in Matthew 20:26–28, often they expect the people with whom they develop relationships to serve and minister to them.

Worship

A third vital church function is worship. Luke writes in Acts 2:42–47 of prayer, the breaking of bread, and praising God. These are vital elements of worship that are commanded elsewhere. For example, Paul instructs the Thessalonians, "Pray continually" (1 Thess. 5:16). And he not only instructs the Corinthians to partake of the Lord's Supper but includes a number of commands as to how to do so (1 Cor. 11:17–34).

Prayer, communion, and praise are forms of worship, as well as giving, singing, and other expressions that attribute worth to God. Luke talks about the "breaking of bread" in verses 42 and 46. Scholars debate whether this was simply a common meal, a meal taken along with communion, or an observance of the Lord's Supper. Because Luke placed it adjacent to teaching, fellowship, and prayer, I believe that he's referring to the Lord's Supper and not simply a meal, though it may have included a meal. While different denominations and organizations may debate its form, most agree the Lord's Supper (1 Cor. 11:23–26) is a primary, critical function of every church that I would include as an aspect of worship.

Evangelism

Evangelism is another vital function of the church. In Acts 2:47 Luke says, "The Lord added to their number daily those who were being saved." Evangelism provides the bookends for this section (vv. 14–47), which begins with Peter's sermon and its results. Of course, evangelism is commanded in other places (see Matt. 28:19–20; 2 Tim. 4:5).

The early churches were very evangelistic, and evangelism was key to the Jerusalem church's outreach into the Jerusalem community and beyond (Acts 1:8). My observation, based on my consulting experience all across North America, is that evangelism is a dying value in the majority of our churches. Back in the twentieth century, some churches, such as the Southern Baptists, were known for their emphasis on evangelism—sometimes to the exclusion of the other functions. According to recent statistics, this is no longer the case. Though not a prophet, I predict that if churches don't begin to value and pursue evangelism, they will experience further decline.

Service

Service or ministry is the final general church function. I find service in Acts 2:45 where Luke writes, "Selling their possessions and goods, they gave to anyone as he had need." Here we see that the early church ministered to its own. In addition, when the church exercised its functions of evangelism and teaching, it also served or ministered to others.

Ministry involves believers in serving God in at least two ways—through the believer's spiritual gifts and through the priesthood of the believer. A spiritual gift is a special, unique capability that God has given all believers to serve him and the body of Christ. Each of us has at least one and likely more spiritual gifts (see 1 Cor. 12:7, 11; Eph. 4:7; 1 Pet. 4:10). The gifts are found primarily in four chapters of the Bible: Romans 12; 1 Corinthians 12; Ephesians 4; and 1 Peter 4. Their operation is vital to the maturing of the body of Christ in each local church (Eph. 4:7–16).

The biblical teaching on the priesthood of the believer is found in such passages as 1 Peter 2:5, 9 and Revelation 1:6; 5:10. In the Old Testament God set aside one tribe (Levi) as his representatives to serve him on behalf of the others. In the New Testament he has called and set aside all believers as his priests to serve him as well as his body, the church. The point is we're all to be involved in ministry in our churches. Service or ministry is necessary and vital to the life of every church.

Other Functions

I have identified five general functions of the church. Other people might disagree with the five I have chosen. Rick Warren, pastor of

Saddleback Church in Southern California—a great church that God has wonderfully blessed—teaches on the Purpose-Driven Church and argues for five purposes of the church: evangelism, worship, fellowship, discipleship, and ministry. His purposes are the same as the church's functions and agree with my five functions. I prefer not to use the term *purpose* because I believe that the church's single purpose biblically and theologically is to glorify God. Warren's point is that believers need to be serving in their churches, and he's correct.

Some suggest other functions of the church, such as miracles and social action. Scott Horrell, who holds to four functions, addresses them in *From the Ground Up*, and I would direct you to his book if you wish to explore this further.[1]

The Church's Five General Functions

Teaching
Fellowship
Worship
Evangelism
Service

The Discovery of Functions

How can we know what is and isn't a function of the church? How can we discover the functions? One way is to use the definition of a function: a timeless, unchanging, and nonnegotiable precept that is based on Scripture and is a mandate for all churches to pursue to accomplish their purpose. All activities of the church can be evaluated against this definition.

There are two other ways to discover the functions of the church. First, functions are ends, not means to ends. Second, they explain why the church does what it does. So when I attempt to discover the church's functions or differentiate between its functions and forms, I ask two questions: Is it an end as opposed to a means to an end? and Why are we doing what we're doing? Actually all the functions do have a common end that I included in the definition above. They must serve the church's purpose, which is to glorify God. However, that's not what I'm addressing here.

Let's revisit some of the functions I listed above. One is worship. Worship is attributing worth to God. Is worship an end in itself? If it means attributing worth to God, then the answer is yes. Let's ask the other question: Why do we worship? The answer is to attribute worth to God. So I feel that worship should be considered one of the church's functions. Another is evangelism. Evangelism is the process of telling the Good News with the goal of winning a lost person to Christ. That's not only an end but answers the question, Why do we evangelize? So it's a function of the church. I'll have more to say about this in the next section on form.

Form

The next *F* in our theology of change is *form*.

The Definition of a Form

I define *forms* as the temporal, changing, and negotiable practices that are based on culture and are methods that all churches are free to choose to accomplish their functions. As you can see, it's practically the opposite of the definition of a function. There are seven characteristics of a church's ministry form.

Temporal or timely

The characteristics of the forms are the opposite of those of the functions. That makes them nonabsolutes. The ones that the first-century church used in ministry may or may not be the same as those the church in the twenty-first century uses. Each church must ask the question, What practices and forms best serve our constituency or the people we desire to reach? Another question is, What forms is God currently using and blessing?

Changing

Whereas functions are unchanging, I would go so far as to say that the forms must change. This is where change takes place in the church. As leaders, pastors can learn from the men of Issachar "who understood the times and knew what Israel should do" (1 Chron. 12:32). Times change and so must our ministry forms if the church is to remain culturally current

> Forms are the temporal, changing, and negotiable practices that are based on culture and are methods that all churches are free to choose to accomplish their functions.

(speaking to people so that they understand our message). Functions never change, but forms must change.

Negotiable

Unlike the functions that aren't negotiable, we can pick and choose the forms that are best for our churches. When they've served their usefulness, we should choose new ones. For example, in some churches, traditional worship has primarily reached the older members (the Builder generation). However, some pastors have negotiated a second service that uses a more contemporary form of worship that enables them to reach the younger generation, who typically have dropped out of church after they complete high school. It's imperative that we realize that a church's style of worship, which reflects its worship form, is an issue of preference, not precept or prescription. Nowhere does the Bible prescribe a particular form of worship!

It's my observation that some theologically liberal churches have reversed function and form. They've treated the biblical functions as temporal, changing, and negotiable, but the cultural forms as timeless, unchanging, and practically nonnegotiable. On the one hand, many have abandoned the faith of the Bible in their attempt to be relevant to modern times. On the other hand, they've clung to old practices that seem to be losing their effectiveness in today's modern world. They lose on both counts and have suffered for it. The mainline denominations have experienced the greatest loss of people of any of our churches during the second half of the twentieth century, and I think this reversal of how they view function and form is part of the reason for their loss.

Cultural

Whereas the basis for the church's functions is the Scriptures, the basis for its forms is culture. If our churches are going to reach the people of this culture, they need to understand the culture. I'll say more about this in the next chapter, but for now let me just say that culture isn't all bad. The typical Christian has been taught intentionally and unintentionally that anything that has to do with culture is worldly and automatically bad. That's simply not the case, and it's a position that doesn't square with Scripture. Culture isn't all bad.

The church expresses or communicates its truths through cultural forms. My argument is that those cultural forms should be understandable and make reasonable sense to those to whom we minister or else we won't communicate. That's certainly true on the mission field. To communicate the gospel to people who speak a language other than English, we have to learn their language, or they won't understand our message. North America is a mission field, and the same truth applies to it.

Involve methods

The functions serve as mandates for the church. However, the forms serve as methods. They are the methods through which the church accomplishes its functions. On the one hand, worship, for example, is a function. On the other hand, a contemporary worship format is a ministry practice or method. The same is true of a traditional format. That's why it is okay to change a church's worship format. As long as you don't jettison the function of worship, you are free biblically to change how you worship. However, you would be wise to prepare and involve the church in such a change, because many people believe that a more contemporary format—using guitars, drums, and other instruments—is wrong and unbiblical, but it's not. Again, as stated above, this is a matter of preference, not precept.

Nonabsolutes

The church's functions are absolutes based on Scripture that serve as mandates for a church's ministry. Thus the implication is that all churches must pursue them in some way rather than some specialty niche. Since the church's forms are nonabsolutes based on culture and serve as methods for its ministry, the implication is that all churches are free to choose the ones they will use. I believe that God has put each church in the driver's seat regarding how it conducts its ministry. This freedom is to be mixed with wisdom and the guidance of the Holy Spirit, however. What a church is free to do and what is wise may not always be the same. I'll say more about freedom below.

Fulfill church's functions

I said before that a church's functions exist to accomplish the church's purpose—to honor and glorify God. And the church's forms exist to accomplish the church's functions. Most people are familiar with the cliché "Form follows function." I would say, "Form serves function." Paul said it this way: "To the weak I became weak, to win the weak. I have become all things to all men so that by all possible means I might save some" (1 Cor. 9:22). This puts the functions where they should be—in the driver's seat. The church identifies the functions and then repeatedly asks, What forms best accomplish each function or what forms is God currently blessing to accomplish a function? Since one of the functions is evangelism, the church asks, How can we best reach lost people? The answer is the various forms or methods for evangelism.

It's important to remember that forms will and should change as the culture changes. While various methods are not bad in themselves, after a little time, they may have served their usefulness. I refer to this as "shelf life." Then it's time to choose another more effective method. The tendency of the typical church, however, is to equate its functions with the cultural forms that it uses to accomplish them and so views the forms as inviolable. When this is the case, change becomes difficult if not impossible, and the church begins to decline. The answer to this problem is for pastors to teach on this topic and train their people to hold their forms with an open hand. A program of regular church evaluation will help churches accomplish this objective. A good audit evaluates the church's methods. I'll say more about evaluation in chapter 10 where I address developing church models.

The Characteristics of Functions and Forms

Functions	Forms
Timeless, unchanging, nonnegotiable (absolute)	Temporal, changing, negotiable (relative)
Based on Scripture	Based on culture
Mandates (ministry precepts)	Methods (ministry practices)
All churches must pursue (found in the Bible)	All churches are free to choose (agree with the Bible)
Accomplish the church's purpose	Accomplish the church's functions

Some Examples of Forms

We've seen in Acts 2:42–47 that the Jerusalem church devoted itself to four primary functions: teaching, fellowship, worship, and evangelism. The fifth, found in other passages of the New Testament, is service. For each function, a number of forms exist to accomplish it.

Let's focus on the function of evangelism. Over the years, churches have developed a number of methods to carry out evangelism. In the New Testament Peter in particular preached several evangelistic messages that resulted in many people coming to the Messiah (see Acts 2:14–41;

3:11–4:4). In the twentieth century, evangelists such as Billy Sunday, D. L. Moody, and Billy Graham used their gifts to conduct evangelistic crusades. Another form of evangelism is confrontational, which involves going door-to-door or confronting people in public places with the gospel. Friendship evangelism is a form that emphasizes the importance of building relationships with people while sharing the gospel with them. Coral Ridge Presbyterian Church in Ft. Lauderdale, Florida, combines confrontation and friendship evangelism (see *Evangelism Explosion*[2]).

At the beginning of the twenty-first century, some of these forms or methods are not as effective as they once were, especially in reaching new, younger generations of North Americans. Thus God is using other methods of evangelism. One is presented in Pastor Steve Sjogren's book *Conspiracy of Kindness*.[3] He and his church are implementing a form of evangelism that involves doing deeds of kindness for unbelievers, expecting and accepting nothing in return. This method of evangelism is most helpful because anyone in the church can do a deed of kindness, such as mowing a neighbor's lawn, washing a car at a free church-sponsored car wash, painting a house, carrying a sack of groceries, or giving away free beverages.

The arrival of the Information Age and the rapid development of information technology, especially the computer, may open up a new frontier for doing evangelism. For example, with the Internet so accessible, some people are developing evangelistic websites.

Examples of Evangelistic Forms

Function	Forms
Evangelism	Crusades
	Door-to-door
	Friendships
	Deeds of kindness
	Websites

Another function of the church is worship. Included under worship is the Lord's Supper—our remembrance of Christ (Matt. 26:26–29; 1 Cor. 11:23–26). I would argue that several different forms are legitimate means for celebrating the Lord's Supper.

I've heard people debate what the proper elements of the Lord's Supper are. Some argue that when Christ instituted the Supper, it was at the time of the Passover; therefore, he must have used unleavened bread that would be equivalent to today's matzo cracker. But note that the passage is descriptive not prescriptive. The Savior commanded that his church observe the Supper in remembrance of him, but he didn't command that we use unleavened bread. The same would be true of what we drink. The passage doesn't command that we use wine or grape juice or some kind of unfermented wine. Some churches elect to use grape juice because a number of their people, especially some new believers, may be recovering alcoholics.

Forms of the Lord's Supper

Function	Forms
Lord's Supper	Grape juice
	Wine
	Matzo crackers
	Bread

The Discovery of Forms

How can we tell the difference between forms and functions? In some cases, it's easy to tell them apart; in others, it's not so easy. To discover the church's functions, I said above that we ask two questions: Is this an end as opposed to a means to an end? and, Why are we doing what we are doing?

To discover forms, we also ask two questions: Is this a means to accomplish an end? Functions are ends, while forms are means to ends. The second question is, How will I implement a particular function? The answer is a form.

Some illustrations should help. We know that baptism is a function because it represents our identity with Christ, which makes it an end in itself. But there are various forms or modes of baptism (immersion and so forth). These forms aren't ends but means to an end. For instance, we don't immerse people simply to be immersing them—that would make immersion an end in itself. Immersion as well as other forms of baptism are means to the end—identification with Christ, which is the meaning of baptism.

The answer to the second question—How will I implement the function, or how will I baptize people?—is the form, such as immersion, sprinkling, pouring, or whatever form you or your denomination accepts.

One other example is the teaching of biblical truth, such as teaching the apostles' doctrine (Acts 2:42). The meaning of teaching in this context is the communication of biblical truth. That's a legitimate end in itself. However, several forms of teaching exist that can be the means to this end. One is the public lecture, as in a church service or some kind of Bible class. Another is teaching through dialogue, where different people teach and there's much interaction. Both of these forms answer the question, How will I teach?

Freedom

The third *F* in the theology of change is *freedom*. We need briefly to explore the implications, limitations, and restrictions of this concept.

Implications

What is the implication for forms? In two places, James clearly states that the Bible, which he calls the "perfect law," gives us freedom (James 1:25; 2:12). This certainly applies to the area of form. All churches under the guidance of the Holy Spirit are free to choose the forms or methods that best accomplish the functions. These forms are nonabsolutes. This means that each church has vast freedom under the Holy Spirit regarding how it implements the functions and ultimately how it does church.

A classic example is using a particular style of music to accomplish the function of worship. Whether a church opts for a traditional or a contemporary form is a matter of preference and the willing submission of one's preference to serve others (Matt. 20:26–28). (If you're a critic of the new church models and you prefer a more traditional or classic format, please resist the urge you're feeling right now to toss this book. Instead, try to think through this issue with me rather than react emotionally.)

Limitations

We limit our freedom and that of others when we assume that there is only one correct way to implement a function such as worship. For example, when we discover the different preferences for worship, we assume that only one is the correct view and begin to search the Scriptures, looking for it. Initially, that's okay. However, after investigating the biblical evidence, if we find that a certain form is not specified, we must be open to the idea that this is a form, not a function, and that several different forms exist for carrying out the function. Remember, we have freedom with nonabsolutes to use the form we choose, provided, of course, that it doesn't violate Scripture.

We must be careful not to vilify others in the exercise of their freedom simply because we don't like the style they choose for worship. This is not only unbiblical but sinful and serves only to divide the body of Christ. I believe that those who willingly follow such an approach should be placed under church discipline as detailed in Matthew 18:15–20.

Restrictions

I propose that there are only two restrictions that affect our freedom to choose forms. The first is that the forms must agree with the Bible. That means that while they may not be found in the Bible, the forms must not contradict or disagree in any way with the teaching of the Bible. That's how we know that the Holy Spirit is involved. The New Testament sets the boundary, and each local church is free under the Holy Spirit to minister within that boundary. The second restriction is that our forms—whether for general or specific functions—must help us accomplish the absolutes and grow in Christ. When this ceases to happen, it becomes imperative that we look for and embrace other more workable forms, even when they may not be our preference.

I close this chapter with an incredibly insightful quote from Francis Schaeffer. In *The Church at the End of the Twentieth Century*, he writes:

> Not being able, as times change, to change under the Holy Spirit is ugly. The same applies to church polity and practice. In a rapidly changing age like ours, an age of total upheaval like ours, to make nonabsolutes absolutes guarantees both isolation and the death of the institutional, organized church.[4]

Questions for Reflection and Discussion

1. How has change affected your church? Has it been good, bad, or a little of both? If you are a pastor or lay leader, what have you done to prepare your people for change?

2. Does your church have a theology of change to guide its change process? If not, why not? If so, what is it? Do people know what it is and understand it?

3. According to the author, what are the five general functions of the church? Evaluate your church in light of each function. Is your church strong in all of them? Are they balanced? If not, where is the church weak? Why? What will you do about it? When?

4. How frequently does your church change its ministry forms? When was the last time your church embraced a new form?

5. How have you handled those who respond negatively and inappropriately to changes in ministry forms?

The Connecting Church

Developing a Theology of Culture

In addition to a theology of change, I contend that twenty-first-century churches must develop a practical, basic theology of culture. Since the church began on the Day of Pentecost, it has needed a theology of culture, and this need will continue as long as the church exists on earth. But do you know of many churches that have articulated a clear, coherent theology of culture? Most pastors—even seminary trained—have never thought through such a theology, so we can expect that the people in their churches have never thought through a theology of culture either. While some have done so intuitively at an unconscious level, most haven't at a conscious level. As globalism increases, and we come into contact with more and different cultures as well as our own, and as new churches appear on the horizon, we will inevitably face practical issues and questions that only a basic, biblical theology of culture can address. For example, how should we as Christians relate to culture? What is culture? What does the Bible say about culture? Is it a friend or an enemy of the church? If anything, what does the

Bible say about the culture of our churches? The answers lie in one's theology of culture.

In this chapter, I'll briefly address five areas that will affect your fundamental thinking about culture. We must explore the reasons culture is so important to us and our churches; we need to define culture and be aware of the various kinds so that we know what we're talking about; we'll discuss how best to respond to culture; we'll explore the relationship between the gospel and culture; and we'll address how the church should relate to culture.

The Importance of Culture

There are four reasons for culture's importance to leaders and their churches.

Culture shapes and influences our life and all of our beliefs. Most people are not aware of the profound influence that culture has on us. But even if we don't realize it, we use culture to order our lives, interpret our experiences, and evaluate behavior. It's our resource for understanding our experiences and making sense of our lives. Since this is largely a mental reflex—an unconscious process—we are hardly aware that it's taking place. It simply happens.

Our cultural presuppositions affect the development of our theology and what we believe about the Bible. Our culture provides a semantic, conceptual framework through which we view God and the Bible. Most of us who are in ministry in evangelical pulpits have been educated under a Western European influence. The institutions where we have trained were heavily influenced by a European system using European theologians. If you recall, Europeans such as Calvin, Luther, Wesley, and others have written or influenced many of the theologies you've read or the commentaries you've followed. In addition, we spent far more time in seminary studying the didactic or teaching books of the Bible than the narrative books. That's very Western, and while it's not bad, it reflects a theological viewpoint developed in the cauldron of a Western European culture.

Our culture affects the way we conduct our ministries in the church. Our own cultural context—both past and present—has shaped much of our practice of the faith as well as our understanding of the faith. From a cultural perspective, many of our older, traditional churches across North America were "made in Europe," whereas the new-paradigm churches were "made in America." For example, European-influenced churches view the church as a building that "looks like a church." That means that the building has arches, possibly columns, and a steeple with a cross on top. Their organization is hierarchical, they emphasize the role and training of the clergy, they're more formal in dress and traditional in worship, they focus more on the past, and their music was written before the 1960s.

Churches that have been influenced primarily by American culture view the church more as people. Their organization is more horizontal, they emphasize the role and training of the laity, they are more casual in dress and contemporary in worship, their focus is on the future, and their music was written after 1960.

At the end of the twentieth century, the European-influenced churches have been in decline, while the American-influenced churches have been growing. In addition, a number of European-influenced churches have experienced a push by their younger people to transition to a more culturally current American-influenced format. This has usually been met with strong resistance, and in some instances, churches have split over it. The problem is that some of these people in the European-influenced churches believe that they are defending the faith when in reality they are defending their cultural heritage. So they fight as if the entire future of orthodox Christianity depends on them. This is most unfortunate and very damaging to the cause of Christ.

Culture helps us understand better the different people we seek to reach for Christ. We live at a time of growing cultural diversity. Consequently, we are reaching out and ministering the gospel to an increasingly multicultural North America. This is happening both within and outside ethnic boundaries. For example, within ethnic boundaries, white Generation Xers live in and experience a different culture than do white Baby Boomers. And both embrace a culture that is totally different from that of their parents and grandparents. So we shouldn't be too surprised when the younger generations fail to embrace the cultural aspects of their parents' and grandparents' Christianity. The same holds true for African Americans, Hispanics, Asians, and others.

Outside ethnic boundaries, America has become a global, multicultural nation. North America isn't a melting pot any longer; it's a salad bowl. We commonly speak of Mexican Americans, African

Americans, and Asian Americans. And in some cities, one of these groups is the dominant racial group, not whites.

Whereas once many North American companies conducted their business only in North America, now many have business interests around the world. Along with improved communication technology, this has brought us into contact with people from all over the world. All this causes the church to ask, How can we best reach these people for Christ?

Four Reasons Why Culture Is Important

- It profoundly shapes and influences our life and all our beliefs.
- It affects the development of our theology and what we believe about the Bible.
- It affects the way we conduct our ministries in the church.
- It helps us understand better the different people we seek to reach for Christ.

The Definition of Culture

What is the definition of *culture*? What are we talking about? When defining a concept, I find it often helpful to talk about what it is and what it isn't. Let's begin by focusing on what culture is.

What Culture Is

Traditional definitions of *culture* usually include such elements as people's thoughts, beliefs, values, speech, actions, and artifacts (man-made objects). These all fall under people's beliefs and actions. Therefore, I define culture as *the sum total of what people believe and how they act on their beliefs.* Culture is the sum of a people's way of life, and it is largely through their culture that people of varying ethnic, social, or religious groups create and make sense of the world they live in. I realize that my definition is broad, so let's examine the two elements that make up the definition.

> Culture is the sum total of what people believe and how they act on their beliefs.

Beliefs

Culture includes people's beliefs. Picture culture as an onion. Its beliefs are at the center of the onion and thus aren't seen. At the core of everyone's beliefs is a worldview. Your worldview consists of your answers to the basic questions of life: What is real? Who are we? Where did we come from? Why are we here? What happens to us at death? What is the basis for morality and ethics? Your answers to these questions inform the assumptions that influence your total belief system. Some Western worldviews are theism, deism, and modernism (naturalism). Currently we are in the midst of a shift from modernism to a new worldview—postmodernism. This view answers the above questions differently than all the former worldviews and will influence the thinking not only of the current generations but of those to come for the next one hundred years or so.

Our worldview dictates what we think and believe is true. We hold our beliefs at two levels. One is our operating beliefs. They are the beliefs that we act on. These beliefs affect and influence our values and overall behavior.

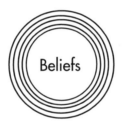

Our theoretical beliefs are the beliefs that we hold at a theoretical level. They may or may not affect our lives. A church's doctrinal statement or creed would be one example of a theoretical belief.

These beliefs are at the heart of our values in general and our actual values in particular. Our values are part of the onion and are the layer that surrounds its inner core of beliefs. Actual values are the beliefs that drive us, that explain why we do what we do. For example, a church's core values, such as evangelism and Bible teaching, drive it, determining what it does. Our actual beliefs also determine what we don't do.

If we truly want to understand a culture, we must get below the surface (the onion's outer peel) and discover the beliefs in general and values in particular of that culture.

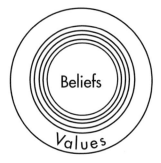

Actions

Culture consists also of people's actions or behavior. We see human behavior at the surface of a culture. When we picture culture as an onion, behavior makes up the outer peel. Our actions are affected by our beliefs and include what we say and do—our language and communication, our activities, and the things we make (artifacts). They include our patterned ways of doing things, such as how we relate to people, our role in society and family, our vocation, where we go, what we read, and the material objects we make, such as clothing, tools, art, and houses. As one old-timer said, "It's how we do things around here!"

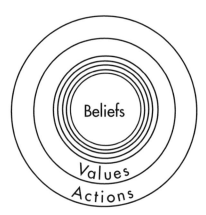

Categories

It also helps our understanding of culture when we learn some of the different categories of culture. One is geographical. Thus we speak of Western culture, Eastern culture, North American culture, urban and suburban culture, and others. Another is philosophical, such as the modern culture and the postmodern culture. A third is ethnic, such as an African American or white culture. There is also institutional or corporate culture—the culture of a business, a school, and a local church, for example.

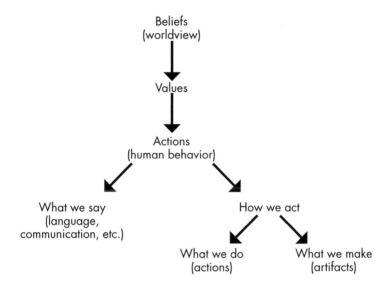

What Culture Isn't

Now that we have a working definition of culture, let's explore what culture isn't. I'm aware of some misconceptions that Christians and churched people hold about culture, which I believe have led to some unfair criticism of church models.

The most common misconception is that culture is inherently evil. I've noted that whenever Christian people, especially well-known teachers and ministry leaders on television and radio, mention culture, it's often in a negative context. Far too many equate it with Satan's world system. When many critics hear someone say that the church needs to be culturally relevant, they interpret that to mean that the church is supposed to be like the world—to buy into and embrace Satan's world system. This represents a total misunderstanding of what the Scriptures teach about culture. Rather than jump to conclusions, it's imperative that we carefully study what God's Word says about these matters. (It is also important that we define our terms for better understanding. In this arena, teachers and leaders must define culture if we are to have an intelligent discussion. However, few do.)

What we must realize is that culture was an intrinsic part of the lives of Adam and Eve before the fall. They had patterns of living in the Garden of Eden (Gen. 2:8–20). Since God created Adam and Eve as thinking and acting persons and created the Garden of Eden, in effect, he created culture. In addition, Genesis 1:31 says, "God saw all that he had made, and it was very good." Thus God created culture and it was very good.

Not only did Adam and Eve think and act, but the Godhead does the same. For example, in Genesis 1 the Godhead's creative acts were the result of creative thought and planning (Acts 4:28). If this is the case, and I think that it's obvious, then the Godhead relates and operates in a cultural context.

Furthermore, the evidence seems to indicate that culture will be an intrinsic part of our future state in heaven. For instance, Revelation 7:9–10 reveals that people's cultural distinctives, such as their ethnicity and language, will be preserved. We see much the same later in Revelation 20–22, specifically Revelation 21:26.

This does not mean, however, that culture is always good. Culture can be good or bad. We see a very different culture after the fall. In essence, the culture was devastated by the fall. Sin pervaded everything including culture (Gen. 3:14–19; 6:5).

We tend to view culture as an end in itself, and this is a problem. Culture is not an end but a means or vehicle to an end. Paul indicates this in Romans 14:14 when he refers to food—a vital aspect of culture—as not unclean in itself, but if someone regards a particular food as unclean, then for him or her it is unclean. Therefore, as a means to an end, food can be used for good or bad. Another example is language. In James 3:9–12 the author distinguishes two uses of the tongue—a figure of speech for language (v. 9). On the one hand, people use it for good, such as praising God. On the other hand, people may use it to curse others who have been created in God's image. Many other things can be used for both good and evil. A hunter can use a gun to provide food for his family, while a criminal may use it to rob a store. The same scalpel can correct a baby's malfunctioning heart valve or take that same baby's life through an abortion.

Our Response to Culture

So far, we have a definition of culture and an understanding that people use culture for good or bad. Next we need to determine a

Christian response to culture that will guide and direct us as we give leadership to our churches—especially new-model churches—that have their own unique corporate cultures. There are three possible responses.

Isolation

Some Christians would say our proper response to culture is isolation, separation from it. Isolationists believe incorrectly that the culture is always inherently evil and an enemy of the gospel. Many would equate it with the term *world* in the Bible and believe that John is warning us to avoid culture in such passages as John 12:31; 16:11; 1 John 4:4; 5:19. Thus they separate themselves from culture. Supposedly, Paul is saying the same in 2 Corinthians 4:4 and Ephesians 2:2.

This call for separation from the world is first-degree separation. Some argue for second-degree separation as well. This view of isolation teaches that Christians must separate not only from the world but from anyone in Christianity that we feel may have compromised the gospel and thus embraced the world. For example, some Christian pastors and other leaders will not associate with Billy Graham and his crusades because he invites some leaders with questionable theology to sit on the platform at his crusades.

I respond to isolationists in several ways. First, the New Testament does use the term *world* for culture. However, that usage refers often to lost people or humanity in general (John 3:16–17, 19; 8:12; 9:5) as dominated by Satan and darkness (12:46). It would also include culture when under the control of Satan, his forces, or men who pursue evil, not good (Eph. 2:2). Isolationists totally miss the biblical teaching on culture as a means for good or bad.

Second, with an isolationist perspective, it is difficult to explain Christ's incarnation. He came into this world, became a man, and embraced the good aspects of the culture.

Third, isolationists view culture as an evil force or object "out there," from which we can separate. However, while culture is "out there," it is also "within us." Not only is culture all around us, it is part of us. The language we speak and the thoughts we think are part of our culture. Our ethnicity is a cultural distinctive. This presents a major dilemma for isolationists. How can you separate from that which is an intrinsic part of who you are?

Accommodation

Accommodation is the other extreme. It is when the Christian accommodates to or adopts the culture.

Theological liberalism seeks to accommodate to culture. It believes that much of the culture is a friend of the gospel and argues that we must adopt the views of modern science, sociology, philosophy, and theology. These views include the acceptance of concepts such as radical feminism, homosexuality, and abortion but would exclude biblical orthodoxy. Since the advocates of accommodation embrace the sinful use of culture, they conform to that culture and buy into the spirit of the age. The problem is that while leaning over to speak to the world, there's a danger you might fall in. And I believe that most liberals have.

There is a conservative form of accommodation, and I'm surprised at the number of Christians who embrace or come very close to embracing this view. It argues unconsciously that God endorses a particular culture or subculture as distinctly Christian. For some it's the first-century culture. Those, for example, who embrace patternism—we should follow the patterns of the first-century churches—tend to believe that God endorses that culture and its practices, which include meeting on the first day of the week and using wine in communion.

Some, such as the Amish, believe that God endorses the culture of the 1800s. So to stay true to that time, they wear black clothing with hooks and eyes rather than buttons and drive a horse and buggy.

Others believe God endorses our twentieth- or twenty-first-century European or North American church culture. Unconsciously we communicate to unbelievers and converts alike that our way of doing things (clothing, singing, temple talk, and especially "doing church") is better than and more Christian than any other way. A common example is when we send the message to unchurched lost people that they have to behave like churched people to be accepted. Many of them think churched people are like Dana Carvey's "church lady" on *Saturday Night Live* in the 1990s. He, or maybe I should say she, has her hair in a bun and wears a dress that extends to her ankles. She doesn't wear any makeup and is quick to tell you what she's against. And she never smiles. Lost people, and I suspect many saved people, don't want any part of that.

When lost unchurched people visit a church, they don't behave like the regulars—they don't know all the cues, such as when to stand and sit, what to wear, how to pray, and so forth. So the regulars think there's something wrong with these visitors. The message we send is that they must become like us and embrace our culture to be accepted and, in some cases, to be saved.

The gospel, however, doesn't presuppose that any culture is superior to another. While some cultures are more advanced than others, the gospel views them not as superior or inferior but as different. We don't have to embrace some distinct Christian culture along with the gospel to be saved. The church determined this at the Jerusalem Council in Acts 15—a Gentile doesn't have to become a cultural Jew (be circumcised and so forth) to be saved! There is nothing that teaches that the first century or the eighteenth century is superior to the twenty-first century. Even though much of the New Testament was written in the first century and the church grew and developed at that time, God doesn't favor or endorse that culture any more than any other culture.

Contextualization

The third possibility and the best response to culture is contextualization, which attempts to plant or reestablish churches within people's cultural context and to communicate the gospel in language and practices that are understandable so that the biblical message is clear. Therefore, contextualization views culture as a means or vehicle that God, man, and Satan can use for their own purposes, whether good or evil. It teaches that a convert doesn't have to adopt or embrace another, so-called Christian or church culture to be accepted, saved, or to join a church. It uses indigenous cultural forms and practices to communicate biblical truth; otherwise, the gospel isn't clear.

Communication and the clarity of the Christian message is what cultural relevance is all about. We must remember that culture communicates. The question is what does it communicate and how clear is the message? Cultural relevance isn't succumbing blindly to some worldly practices, as some argue, but understanding a culture well enough to articulate and communicate to the people of that culture in a way that they hear and, with the aid of the Holy Spirit, understand the gospel. To fail to be culturally relevant is to muddy the gospel with unnecessary cultural trappings that serve only to miscommunicate the Christian message. While our missionaries in foreign lands understand this (they learn the language, for example), some of our churches in North America have totally missed it. Some even argue that cultural relevance is fine for the mission field but not in North America. Not only does this make absolutely no sense, but it demeans missions.

Though God is above and beyond human culture, he has chosen to work through our culture and even, at times, to limit himself to that culture. For example, he chose to speak to men, such as Adam, Moses, and the prophets, through human language. Had he used some heavenly language (1 Cor. 13:1), they wouldn't have understood him.

Jesus's incarnation is a great example of contextualization. He incarnated himself in a human body, learned a language, and lived among and learned from people (Luke 2:52). One reason he did this was to reveal himself to humankind in a way that communicated clearly to them. As he lived and spoke the message, they got it.

Finally, Paul, rather than impose his own culture on those to whom he ministered, chose instead to adapt to them and the morally acceptable elements of their culture. In 1 Corinthians 9:19–22 he teaches:

> Though I am free and belong to no man, I make myself a slave to everyone, to win as many as possible. To the Jews I became like a Jew, to win the Jews. To those under the law I became like one under the law (though I myself am not under the law), so as to win those under the law. To those not having the law I became like one not having the law (though I am not free from God's law but am under Christ's law), so as to win those not having the law. . . . I have become all things to all men so that by all possible means I might save some.

Three Responses to Culture

Isolation	Accommodation	Contextualization
Attempts to withdraw from culture	Embraces either a sinful use of culture or a particular culture as uniquely Christian	Uses indigenous cultural practices to clearly communicate biblical truth and make the gospel clear

Culture and the Gospel

What is the relationship between the gospel and culture? Is the gospel above or part of the culture? How should the church relate to the gospel and culture? The church in North America needs to answer these and other questions about the gospel and culture to accomplish Christ's mission.

Supracultural and Cultural

We must remember that the gospel is supracultural in its origin and essence but cultural in its interpretation and application. God, who transcends man's culture and is thus supracultural, is the source of the gospel (Gal. 1:11–12; 2 Tim. 3:16). However, Christians originally recorded and communicated the gospel in the context of the Greco-Roman culture. Today we interpret, study, and apply the gospel in the context of other cultures, such as North American, European, and Asian. Therefore, we must understand that though supracultural in function, the gospel exists in some cultural context. And an understanding of that culture enhances the clarity of the gospel.

Distinguishing between the Gospel and Culture

It is imperative that Christians and churches distinguish between the gospel and their culture. Failure to make a distinction between the gospel and culture mixes the two together in people's minds and communicates that acceptance of the gospel also includes the acceptance of certain cultural practices, such as singing the great hymns of the faith played on a piano or organ; wearing formal clothing, such as coats, ties, and long dresses; or even wearing your hair in a bun. And the same is true of a contemporary cultural mind-set as well. There were some people in the early church who failed to make this distinction. They argued that a believer had to observe the custom of circumcision to be saved (Acts 15:1).

Using Culture to Clarify the Gospel

We must discover how to use our culture and that of others to clarify and promote the gospel. When we put the gospel into other people's cultural forms, whether North American or some other, we make it possible for them to understand it, embrace it, and communicate it to others. Therefore, we should seek to express the gospel in ways and forms that our target group—unchurched, lost North Americans, lost Asians, lost Javanese, and others—can understand. However, we must be sure that the cultural forms we use convey the proper message. For example, the use of wine as a part of communion in some contexts could convey a negative message. The same could be true of the use of drums and guitars in a worship service populated mostly by the Builder generation.

Some Implications of Culture and the Gospel

- The gospel is supracultural in its origin and essence but cultural in its interpretation and application.
- It is imperative that Christians and churches distinguish between the gospel and their culture.
- We must discover how to use our culture and that of others to best clarify and promote the gospel.

Culture and the Church

A proper understanding of culture, the gospel, and the Scriptures teaches us much about how we do church. What are some of these lessons? Let's look at several.

Culture Affects All Churches

Culture affects all churches. There are no exceptions. The question, therefore, isn't, Does culture affect what we do as a church? Rather, the question is, Which culture primarily affects what we do as a church? Most older, established white churches in North America still reflect a Western European culture. Their practices and customs were made in Europe. Actually, Christian churches are among the few institutional vestiges of European culture that are still standing in America. Cultural practices such as the use of organ music, hymns, altars, pews, collection plates, kneelers, stained-glass windows, a distinct architecture, and robes are Western European, not biblical, in origin. Much the same is true of the newer paradigm churches that have rejected the influence of European culture. Instead, they have adopted different cultural practices that are American, not biblical, in origin. They are churches that are made in America.

This isn't necessarily bad. Remember that culture is a means that can be used for good or bad. If the people in our churches cling to a European culture as if it were a biblical culture and refuse to adjust when the culture all around them is changing, then it could be bad. When the church's culture, not the message, unnecessarily turns people off to the gospel and Christianity, then it is bad. Unfortunately, far too many of our churches did this, consciously and unconsciously, at the end of the twentieth century. Now unchurched people visit a church and often find that it's a culturally alienating experience. They don't understand the jargon ("temple talk"), can't relate to the music, and feel uncomfortable and out of place. Thus they conclude wrongly that Christianity and the gospel aren't for them. Add to this the practice in some churches that requires lost people to behave like churched people before the church will accept them, and you have a formula for spiritual disaster. That's a big part of what Acts 15 corrected in the first century, and today's twenty-first-century churches must do likewise. They must not confuse culture with biblical precept.

The Extensive Impact of Culture

Culture affects our churches more than we realize. I'm convinced that as much as 80 to 90 percent of what we do in our churches is culturally, not biblically, directed. An example is church music. It plays a far greater role than most realize, not only in the lives of our adults but in the lives of our young people. This has been true in the past and will be true in the future. Musicians and their music exert a profound influence on today's youth culture. To ignore this or not be aware of it in our churches is to risk the alienation and loss of our youth to the cause of Christ. People in our churches have to realize that today's traditional music was yesterday's contemporary music, and today's contemporary music is tomorrow's traditional music. For an older generation to impose their tastes on the younger generations—no matter how innocently—means that both groups suffer in the long term. Those in the church must let the newer generations develop styles and a culture that best convey Christianity to them, as long as they don't clash with Scripture.

The problem is that most pastors and congregations aren't aware of this. They believe that if they change something, they are somehow violating Scripture, not just changing the church's culture. As one deacon quipped, "If the organ was good enough for Jesus and Paul, then it better be good enough for us!"

For others, unfortunately, power is the issue. They have the power in the church, and they want to keep things the way they are. Regardless, the good news is that each church has a lot to say regarding its culture. It can choose to make changes in its culture that enhance, not hinder or compromise, the clarity of the gospel.

My advice to older pastors of established churches is to be a student of the culture. Though I'll say more about this below, it means that you'll need to be a learner as well as an instructor—a listening head as well as a talking head. It's imperative that you take time out of your busy schedule to listen and observe. In particular, learn what the younger generations are listening to, watching, and saying. You don't have to agree with it, simply be aware of it to the point that you can articulate it and discuss it with others. Next, be willing to lay your cultural forms on the altar. If culture is a means or vehicle to an end, when culture no longer communicates—especially to a younger generation—shouldn't you be willing to work to make changes? I would argue that the older generations, not the younger ones, should set the example here, and without the help of the older generations, this may not happen.

Finally, do everything within your power to work together with the younger people in the church. Let's face it, they are the future of your church. Without them your church has no future. Someone has said, "The family that prays together stays together." In the cultural context I would argue, "The church family that pulls together stays together." If we don't pull together, we'll pull apart.

Some People Excluded

Our church cultures will exclude some people. Most of us in general and younger Christians in particular desire to reach everyone, and that's good. However, I believe it was Peter Wagner who said a church that attempts to reach everyone in general will likely reach no one in particular. Face it, your church's culture will exclude some people—it can't be helped. Keep in mind that we're talking about lost people as well as saved people. Some simply will not care for your church's style of music and so on. In effect, they're rejecting you. My point is that it is okay not to reach everybody. That's why so many different kinds of churches exist. It takes all kinds of churches to reach all kinds of people, and this is a powerful argument for new-model churches! The important things are that we're *willing* to reach everyone, we don't needlessly turn people off to the gospel, and not only are we open to new-paradigm churches but we are promoting them.

Now the question becomes, Who will we reach? Keep in mind that I'm talking about unbelievers more than believers (though the same applies to believers). We will reach the people who are attracted to us and to our culture, those, for example, who like our style of church in general. While there will be some exceptions, this is the norm. Therefore, those who are culturally attracted to us could form our initial target group. Just as Paul targeted the Gentiles and Peter targeted the Jews (Gal. 2:7), so we'll target certain people as well.

No Superior Culture

No culture is distinctively Christian and thus superior to another. While I've already commented on this earlier, it bears repeating. God hasn't endorsed any culture as uniquely Christian. He has not put his stamp of approval on any of them. The Bible in no way encourages us to strive to be like the first century or any other century.

As we have seen, some include—knowingly or unknowingly—their particular culture as a prerequisite for salvation, along with the gospel. Usually these cultures look strangely Western, some prerequisite cultures are denominational, and many smack of capitalistic, middle-class American values. Though some of these values are good, we must be careful to distinguish between a Christian use of culture and labeling a culture as Christian.

Remaining Relevant

The church that exegetes its culture as well as the Scriptures should remain relevant to that culture. Like the men of Issachar, we should understand our times so that we know how to communicate well and reach people (1 Chron. 12:32). Exegeting our culture helps us to understand it, to discern what is good and bad about it and how to minister well to those who are a part of it. How do you exegete the culture? I suggest five steps.

1. Build redemptive friendships with lost people. Don't be surprised if they don't seek you out. You'll have to seek them out, much as the Savior came to do (see Luke 19:10). Invite your lost next-door neighbor to jog with you around the park or play some basketball. Watch a video with a lost friend. Always be sensitive to and looking for opportunities to present the gospel. Here's a vital question: If someone were to take a snapshot of you and your friends, would there be any lost faces in the photograph?
2. The next step is to attempt to listen hard and well when people talk to you. That way you gain insight into who they are, their interests, where they're struggling in life, and their concern for spiritual matters.

3. Try to read a lot. While watching my favorite college and professional football teams on television, I'm also reading the newspaper, magazines, books, or surfing the Internet. I want to know what my neighbors are reading and the ideas they are exposed to. You would benefit from doing the same.

4. Collect demographic and psychographic information about your community. Demographics is general information about people—where they live, their education, marital status, and so on. Psychographics is what they value and how it influences their lifestyles. This information tells you much about the culture of your community.

5. On occasion, conduct a community survey where you ask people such questions as: Are you currently attending a church? What do you think is the greatest need in the community? Why don't more people attend church? What should churches do to reach people?

Culture and the Church

- Culture affects all churches.
- Culture affects our churches more than we realize.
- Our church cultures will exclude some people.
- No culture is distinctly Christian and superior to all the rest.
- The church that exegetes the culture will be able to remain relevant to that culture.

Questions for Reflection and Discussion

1. Did the author manage to convince you that culture is important to the church? If so, which arguments were the most influential? If not, why not?

2. What was the author's definition of culture? Do you agree with this definition? If not, why? How might this definition help you to understand culture better? What is your definition?

3. Do you agree with the author's position that culture in itself is neutral and may be used for good or bad? Why or why not? Do you equate culture with the world as defined in Scripture? Why or why not?

4. Of the three responses to culture, which best describes that of your ministry? Why? Has this always been your view? Why or why not? How does your current response help you to do church?
5. Do you believe that culture affects all churches? If not, why? If so, how has it affected yours? Name some ways.
6. Have you found that your church's culture consciously or unconsciously excludes some people? If so, then who and why?
7. Do you agree that no culture is necessarily Christian or superior to another? Why or why not? If not, what is a culture that you believe is Christian or superior?
8. Do you agree with the author's understanding of cultural relevance, or do you believe that for a church to be culturally relevant, it has to embrace the world? Why is it so important to him that churches be culturally relevant?
9. What are some aspects of your church's culture that might unnecessarily turn believers and unbelievers away? What will you do about this?

Defining Church

Developing a Definition of the Local Church

Throughout this book, as I've used the term *church*, I've assumed that you understand what I mean. However, that's not a good assumption to make for your sake as well as mine. So it's time to work toward a definition of the local church. A definition is important not only for clear communication, but to help leaders gauge when a church has gone too far or not far enough, and might not legitimately be considered a church. With all the new models that are out there and the ones to come, how can we know if they are legitimate New Testament churches? When is an organization a church? And can a church cease to be a church?

The New Testament doesn't provide us with a definition of the local church, and that may be intentional. The authors were writing letters, not textbooks, to churches and to those who worked with them (Timothy and Titus). To develop a definition we must look at the different biblical characteristics of a church and arrive at a definition based on them.

I would categorize such a definition as an important nonessential, not an essential as based on the discussion in chapter 3. While a definition of the church is necessary for evaluating different models, we must be careful not to say that our definition is the biblical definition or the only correct one. We must never be guilty of condemning others because their definition doesn't precisely align with ours.

The New Testament seems to identify certain elements that make up a legitimate, practical, and biblical local church. Note for a moment the four adjectives I have just used to modify the word *church*.

1. *Legitimate.* We must ask these questions: When is an organization a church? When is it not a church or when might it cease to be a church?
2. *Practical.* We need a definition that is practical and will help us not only serve God's purpose here on earth but answer the questions I just asked. Also, revisiting afresh what our local church is all about can breathe new life into some of our struggling, dying churches. It also needs to be practical in the sense that it's a working definition. We can use it to critique what we're doing and ask, Are we functioning as a local church?
3. *Biblical.* The definition needs to be biblical. Again, while Scripture doesn't define the church, it does provide us with some attributes of a church.
4. *Local.* We want to define the local church. We may also view the church universally. The universal church consists of all believers in all the churches together around the world and is made up of all the local churches. My focus isn't on the universal church but the local form of it.

Early in the 1500s, the reformers in the Protestant church developed a definition for *church*. The Lutheran, Calvinistic, and Anglican traditions believed the churches consisted of two characteristics. First, the church is where the Word of God is proclaimed, and second, it is where the sacraments are correctly taught and administered. This is helpful but doesn't go far enough. Its focus is totally inward and ignores other critical aspects of the church, such as evangelism and the church's mission. If this definition were correct, then a Bible study in a college dorm could be a church.

I've built my definition of the local church around both its being and its doing: the church both *is* and *does*. It is or exists as something and acts or does something. Here is my definition: I believe that *a local church is an indispensable gathering of professing believers in Christ who, under leadership, are organized to pursue its mission through its functions to accomplish its purpose.* The rest of the chapter will articulate and examine seven critical elements that make up this definition.

Indispensable

The first element in my definition is that the church is indispensable. I mean by this that the local church is God's only divinely sanctioned institution to reach the world for Christ. Thus it is an essential, vital institution. Bill Hybels means this when he says that the church is the hope of the world. He's merely echoing the Savior, who said to Peter, "I will build my church, and the gates of Hades will not overcome it" (Matt. 16:18). The reason this is so important is reflected in Barna's research that I cited in chapter 1 of this book. As you recall, he noted that a growing number of committed Christians are dropping out of their churches altogether because they believe that church is doing them more harm than good. Based on the New Testament teaching on the church, I have serious problems with those who drop out of church altogether. Jesus teaches us that the church is so important to his plans for humankind that we should be a part of one. If attendance in a church is hampering our spiritual development, then we should be a part of planting a spiritually healthy church. But we can't abandon the church based on our experience in a spiritually unhealthy situation.

Other Christians have chosen to remain in a spiritually weak church and supplement their experience with involvement in a parachurch ministry. Certainly this is better than simply dropping out of church. Parachurch ministries have sprung up primarily to make up for the deficiencies of the local church. It's imperative, however, that they not attempt to take the place of the church or work against it in any way. To do so is to oppose Christ and his building his church (Matt. 16:18). I would challenge believers in this situation to turn all their attention to revitalizing their weak churches. If these churches repeatedly over time refuse to move forward, then it's time to find a new church or become involved in a church plant.

> The local church is an indispensable gathering of professing believers in Christ who, under leadership, are organized to pursue its mission through its functions to accomplish its purpose.

A Gathering of Professing Believers in Christ

The second element of the definition is that the church is a gathering of professing believers in Christ, and this is partly the reason it is called a church. The English word *church* translates the Greek word *ekklesia*, which is found in the New Testament, as in 1 Thessalonians 1:1 and many other places. It carries the general meaning of an assembly. Another similar term is *sunago*, which means "gathering" and is used when referring to the church in Acts 14:27: "On arriving there, they gathered (*sunago*) the church together and reported all that God had done through them and how he had opened the door of faith to the Gentiles." Thus the local church is an assembly or gathering of people. This means that one person isn't the church. It takes at least two people to make a church. Also it's the assembled or gathered people who make up the church, not a building or some other organization. Prior to my definition above, I said that the church both is and does. Here the stress is on the local church as it is. What is it? It is people.

For a long time I assumed that the church consisted of people who are believers in Christ, those who had at some point in time accepted Christ as Savior. However, I can distinctly remember one Sunday when one of the deacons in the church I attended came to faith in Christ. All of us were shocked to think that a man in such a position might not be a believer in Christ. Everyone assumed he was. George Barna has warned in the past that every local church, even evangelical churches, has unbelievers who are part of its people. And he warns that likely there are more of them than most people realize.

The realization that unbelievers were present in the church didn't influence my definition as much as my doctoral work with Dr. Charles Ryrie at Dallas Seminary. One day in a doctoral class, we were discussing what the Bible said about the local church. He asked us to define the local church, and most of us included believers in our definitions. Then he asked how the presence of unbelievers in the church would affect our definitions. Would a church with unbelievers cease to be a church? We all quickly changed our definitions to allow for the presence of non-Christians. As you can see, I chose to use the word *professing* to signal this.

Obviously we would want and expect our churches to be made up of Christians. However, the parable of the wheat and tares (Matt. 13:24–30) warns us that the kingdom of heaven (a reference to a future time here on earth) is made up of unbelievers as well as believers. We shouldn't be surprised that the same is true for Christ's church on earth. In addition, this is a good argument for having church membership, because such a process allows the church to examine its attenders to determine if they are true believers or unbelievers.

Under Leadership

The church is an indispensable gathering of professing believers in Christ who are under leadership. Leadership is vital to the spiritual health of every church. You might think that preaching is the most important aspect of the church. Preaching is important, and seminaries tend to emphasize it over everything else, including leadership. I want to be clear. Preaching is vital to the life of any church, and it is most important that those who preach in our churches preach well, because they are communicating God's message to humankind. I write this not to put down seminaries or preaching, but the truth is that the church rises or falls on leadership. I would argue that a major reason so many churches are struggling today is that many pastors aren't leaders. They may also be poor communicators, which is another reason for a church to struggle.

The writer of Hebrews reflects on the importance of leadership when first he urges his readers to remember their leaders and then to imitate their faith (Heb. 13:7). In verse 17 he directs them: "Obey your leaders and submit to their authority."

The New Testament presents two offices of leadership in the church—elders and deacons.

Elders

After the apostles the elders were the primary leaders in New Testament churches. They are mentioned in a number of places (Acts 14:23; 15:2, 22; 20:17; 1 Tim. 5:17; Titus 1:5; James 5:14; and 1 Pet. 5:1). As I mentioned in chapter 4, I believe that the elders were the first-century pastors of the house churches, which would occasionally gather together as the city church. I won't take space here to develop this view. If you would like to know more, see my book *Being Leaders*.[1] In 1 Timothy 3:1–7 and Titus 1:5–9, Paul provides the church with the necessary qualifications for an elder.

As pastors and leaders of local house churches, elders served their flocks through three universal, timeless functions: protection, teaching, and direction or leadership. These elder-pastors protected their congregations from false teaching. Thus Paul commands the Ephesian elders, "Keep watch over yourselves and all the flock of which the Holy Spirit has made you overseers" (Acts 20:28). First Timothy 5:17 indicates that some, not all, elders preached and taught their people. The ability to teach is also one of the qualifications for being an elder, according to 1 Timothy 3:2. Finally, a third timeless function of an elder is leading the congregation. According to 1 Timothy 5:17, they served to "direct the affairs of the church."

The New Testament also teaches in Romans 12:8 that there's a spiritual gift of leadership. It makes sense, therefore, that an important qualification for elders and deacons is that they have the leadership gift.

Deacons

In addition to the elders, there were also deacons in the New Testament churches. The English word *deacon* means "servant." Deacons were an officially recognized group that are mentioned only twice in the Bible. Paul refers to the overseers (elders) and deacons, who were a part of the church at Philippi (Phil.1:1). He also presents their qualifications immediately following those of elders in 1 Timothy 3:8–10. Some believe that the seven men described in Acts 6:1–6 were deacons in the Jerusalem church. However, there is no conclusive evidence that these men were deacons. Also there is no Scripture that enjoins the church to elect or appoint deacons. Thus their presence seems optional.

Because Scripture doesn't provide much information about the deacons, we can only speculate about what they did. The meaning of the term implies that they served the church in some way as leaders. Most believe that they served under the elders and in a more practical and less official capacity.

Today it's not uncommon for churches to exist without one or both of these offices. However, there will be some leadership in the church, most likely at a lay level. We seem to be wired in such a way that intuitively we seek leadership, so there are no true leaderless situations. People won't let this happen. Either they promote someone (such as a matriarch or patriarch) unofficially to the position, or someone will rise to the occasion. This doesn't negate, however, the truth that every church needs gifted, godly leadership at both a pastoral and lay level.

An Organization

The local church is an indispensable gathering of professing believers in Christ who are under leadership and are organized. Organization involves bringing structure to something. The church is a gathering of people that has organization. Some don't like the truth that the church isn't only an organism but also an organization. Others struggle more with the amount of organization, ranging from very little to a lot. Scripture affirms organization in general and doesn't really address the amount. I'm convinced that no church can exist without some degree of organization. The goal is to hit a happy medium for your ministry. Too much structure stifles creativity and may block effective communication, whereas too little frustrates those who need boundaries.

It may seem strange that I would have to support the need for organization in the church, but for those who might question it, here is some evidence that the church was and should be organized.

1. As we just saw above, the New Testament church organized its leadership under the offices of elders and deacons.
2. Churches were to worship in an organized fashion. Paul tells the Corinthian church: "But everything should be done in a fitting and orderly way" (1 Cor. 14:40).
3. The way that churches were organized along the lines of church government appears to have affected how they handled power. (It's possible that all three forms of church government—Episcopal, Presbyterian, and congregational—were observed in some way in the first century.)
4. The Jerusalem church organized its meetings to take place in homes (Acts 2:46; 8:3) and larger contexts (2:46; 3:11).
5. The church was organized in its practice of the ordinances of baptism (2:41) and the Lord's Supper (vv. 42, 46).
6. The church organized to help its people who were in need (2:45; 4:32).

Pursuing a Mission

The local church is an indispensable gathering of professing believers in Christ who, under leadership, are organized to pursue its mission. The church's mission is and always has been the Great Commission

(Matt. 28:19–20; Mark 16:15). The following chart summarizes the various passages that address the Great Commission.

The Great Commission

Scripture	Directed to Whom	What	Ministry to Whom	How	Where
Matt. 28:19–20	Eleven disciples	Go, make disciples.	All nations	Baptizing and teaching	——
Mark 16:15	Eleven disciples	Go, preach the Good News.	All creation	——	All the world
Luke 24:46–48	Eleven disciples	Be witnesses.	All nations	Preaching repentance and forgiveness of sins	Beginning in Jerusalem
Acts 1:8	Eleven disciples	Be my witnesses.	——	With power	Jerusalem, Judea, Samaria, and the uttermost parts of the world

Based on this chart, we can say that Christ's Great Commission for his church is its mission—to go and make and mature disciples. The going means that the church must be proactive in its attempts to reach people. In Acts 1:12–14 we find the church huddled together in an upper room. This didn't last long as they began to act on Jesus's last words: "But you will receive power when the Holy Spirit comes on you; and you will be my witnesses in Jerusalem, and in all Judea and Samaria, and to the ends of the earth" (v. 8). Making disciples is evangelism, and maturing those disciples is edification.

The success of today's churches, whether new- or old-paradigm, is measured by their obedience to this Great Commission. My experience is that too many of the older paradigm churches, perhaps as many as 80 to 85 percent, view themselves as a family who are responsible to take care of their own people, and they hire a pastor as a chaplain to do this for them. This raises the question: Are they really a church? Can you be a missionless church? I'm convinced that every church has a mission, whether they know it or not. Since they have core values, those values will guide them toward a mission. It may not be the Great

Commission but some aspect of it, such as evangelism, Bible teaching, worship, or simply an inward focus on taking care of one another and the elderly members.

But is a church that ignores the Great Commission a church? If you define the church broadly (and that's what I've done), then it is. Just because it's a disobedient church doesn't mean it isn't a church. Just because I'm a disobedient Christian doesn't mean I'm not a Christian. However, if a church has no intention of pursuing the Great Commission as specifically articulated by the Savior, I would question whether it is truly a church, at least from a biblical perspective. This would be true of some of the mainline churches that don't profess to believe or follow the Scriptures. They don't meet an essential core ingredient of a New Testament church.

Functions

The local church is an indispensable gathering of professing believers in Christ who, under leadership, are organized to pursue its mission through its functions. The church's functions are critical to its fulfilling the Great Commission. Functions are the church's means to accomplish the church's mission. I've defined the functions earlier in chapter 5 as the timeless, unchanging, and nonnegotiable precepts that are based on Scripture and are mandates for all churches to pursue to accomplish their purpose. In the same chapter, I divided the church's functions into two categories—general and specific. The church must provide and practice the general functions if its people are to become mature. Thus the general functions are for all believers. The specific functions, such as leadership, are for certain but not all congregants. I argue that the church has five functions: teaching, fellowship, worship, evangelism, and service or ministry as based on Acts 2:42–47 and other prescriptive passages covered in chapter 5.

The problem is that some churches are acting like parachurch ministries and have made one of the functions their mission. They've replaced Christ's mission with a favorite function. So, for example, the mission of some churches is teaching—they believe that their church's mission is to teach the Word. Others believe that their mission is to evangelize, or worship, or pursue fellowship or service. I believe that their emphasis is based on the core values that drive them. Those that value teaching the Scriptures do just that but often fail to pursue one or several of the other functions.

Again the question is, Are they legitimate, biblical churches? I believe that the answer is yes. My argument is the same as above. Because they don't pursue the Great Commission and replace it with a function, they are disobedient to Christ and his Word. However, that doesn't mean that they cease to be a church. It makes them a disobedient church. I'm well aware that this last statement will be a shock to some in these churches. Many really believe they are doing God's will by emphasizing one of the functions. I've seen this in the Teaching Church or Bible Church Movement. Regardless of how people respond, we must acknowledge that Scripture teaches clearly that the church's mission is the Great Commission, and we must attempt to balance the five functions of the church, not single out one and make it our sole mission.

Purpose

Purpose is the last element in the definition of a church. The local church is an indispensable gathering of professing believers in Christ who, under leadership, are organized to pursue its mission through its functions to accomplish its purpose. Every organization has a purpose for its existence, whether it knows it or not. As stated earlier in this book, the church's purpose is to glorify God. As it performs its functions and fulfills the Great Commission in its ministry community, it accomplishes its purpose. God is glorified.

Again, I must ask, If the church fails to accomplish its purpose, does it cease to be a church? I think not. To some degree, as in the other cases above, this kind of church is a disobedient church, but its disobedience doesn't disqualify it from being a legitimate, New Testament church. Also, as the church accomplishes one or several of its functions, I suspect that it brings some glory to God. It may be that an organization does not purpose to be a church. It may have an entirely different purpose for its existence. That is why purpose is so important to a ministry organization. This would be true of parachurch organizations that profess a different purpose for their existence—evangelism, teaching, or some other purpose.

In conclusion, I believe that we must have and then apply a working definition of a biblical church to older model churches, existing new-model churches, and those new models that are sure to come in the future. Some of our current established churches will meet this definition, and some won't, which is cause for self-examination and correction. The new models and those in the future will likely use different forms and ways of doing ministry to accomplish their functions. The definition of a church will serve as a litmus test to determine if these are biblical or nonbiblical churches. It must be the definition and not our personal opinions, preferences, or prejudices that determine how we respond to these churches. Just because they don't do church the way we're used to doesn't mean we should criticize and dismiss them.

Questions for Reflection and Discussion

1. Before reading this chapter, did you have a definition for the local church? If not, why not? If so, what is it?
2. Do you agree with the author's definition? Why or why not? How has his definition affected your definition? What might you add or leave out?
3. Do you believe that there's a point that a church can reach that disqualifies it from being a church? If so, what is that point? Do you agree or disagree with the author's view on this?
4. How might a definition of the local church help you as you examine both old- and new-paradigm churches?
5. How does your church compare with the author's definition of a church? What are the differences and similarities? How crucial are they to your church? Will you seek to change anything in your church?
6. How will you respond to future church models? According to the author, how should you respond? Do you agree or disagree with him? Why?

8

The Serving Church

The Biblical Concept of Servanthood

One topic that is lukewarm in far too many of our North American churches early in the twenty-first century is servanthood. Both the Old and New Testaments supply us with a rich resource of passages that address the importance of servanthood in the lives of God's people. My goal in this chapter is to focus specifically on the teachings of Jesus and Paul on servanthood and apply them to today's churches. My contention is that if today's churches are to be biblical, they must be examples of servanthood, not only to each other but especially to their lost and dying communities.

First, we'll briefly look at the teaching of Jesus on servanthood found in Matthew 20:20–28 and then the teaching of Paul, specifically in 1 Corinthians 9:19–23. Second, I'll show how three modern-day churches have implemented this concept of servanthood in their ministry to lost people.

Jesus's Teaching on Servanthood

The Context of Servanthood in Matthew 20:20–28

Before we examine what Jesus says about servanthood, it's important that we look at the context surrounding this core passage. A cardinal rule for interpreting the Bible is that we look at a passage in its context. Most false teaching is the result of taking a passage out of its context. As I noted in an earlier chapter, when you violate its context, you can make the Bible say anything you want.

The context for Jesus's teaching in Matthew 20 begins in Matthew 18:1. Matthew writes: "At that time the disciples came to Jesus and asked, 'Who is the greatest in the kingdom of heaven?'" This passage too has a context that will help us understand the disciples' question. It is found in Mark 9:33. Here Jesus asks the disciples a question that discloses what was on their minds: "They came to Capernaum. When he was in the house, he asked them, 'What were you arguing about on the road?' But they kept quiet because on the way they had argued about who was the greatest."

Somewhere along the way they had missed what their journey was all about. It wasn't about them, the twelve disciples; it was all about him, the Savior. They had become focused on themselves and not him. In particular, they were concerned about their individual, personal greatness to the point that the discussion had turned ugly. Apparently each one took a turn telling the others the reasons he was better and more deserving than they were. They were so blinded to their own lack of humility that they went to Jesus with the question, "Who is the greatest in the kingdom of heaven?" Based on the context of Mark 9:33, I suspect they were asking, "Which one of *us* is the greatest in the kingdom of heaven?" And much to their surprise, Jesus turned to a little child and gave them a lesson in humility (Matt. 18:2–9).

Based on other passages in the chronology of events, the disciples didn't get it. For example, next, in the context of Matthew 20, Peter responds to the Savior's teaching on the kingdom of heaven in Matthew 19:16–26. Jesus has just taught a rich man who would not humble himself a lesson in humility, and Peter answers, "We have left everything to follow you! What then will there be for us?" Here is my translation of Peter's question: "We have left everything to follow you! Now what's in it for us?" or "What are we going to get out of it?" Again, it's all about them and not Jesus. What is interesting is that rather than rebuke Peter, in verses 28–30, Jesus answers his question and teaches that someday in his kingdom, they will have special positions of leadership.

Another issue of context that will help us understand Jesus's concept of servanthood is found in Matthew 20:17–19. In this passage Jesus teaches the disciples what is about to happen to him. He states that he will be betrayed, condemned, mocked, flogged, and crucified. This is hardly what they expected. They were looking for a kingdom, not a cross. Again they didn't understand, and the following scene takes place when the mother of James and John comes to Jesus and asks him to place her sons in the top positions of leadership and authority in his coming kingdom. You would hope that they would be more concerned about his future on a cross. They weren't. Their concern was their future on a throne, probably keying off Jesus's words to Peter in Matthew 19:28–30.

You must realize that not only was this woman the mother of James and John, but some believe she may have been Jesus's aunt (see Matt. 10:2; 27:56). Possibly this was one member of Jesus's family taking advantage of her position. James and John wanted to sit at Jesus's right and left in his kingdom—positions of prestige and power, where they and not the other disciples would share in his authority and preeminence. When word got back to the other ten disciples, they were upset (20:24). These two with their mother had attempted to use their kinship to their advantage, wanting to be the greatest in the kingdom of heaven.

The Concept of Servanthood in Matthew 20:20–28

With this context in mind, we can better understand Jesus's response in Matthew 20:25–28 to the disciples' reaction. Things had obviously gotten out of hand. It was time for a vital midcourse correction in their thinking. These disciples were to be prominent kingdom leaders, but they would also be humble servants. Jesus follows with a lesson on servant leadership. In the passage, he teaches that greatness in his kingdom involves humility, service, and a focus on others.

Leading with Humility

Matthew 20:25–26 says, "Jesus called them together and said, 'You know that the rulers of the Gentiles lord it over them, and their high officials exercise authority over them. Not so with you.'" Jesus is teaching his disciples that servant leaders lead humbly. They're characterized as humble or selfless leaders. The disciples needed to hear this because they were full of themselves. They had to learn to lead with humility, not focusing on their ego or themselves.

Some might feel that Jesus is speaking out against authority in this passage and saying that the disciples weren't to lead with authority. That isn't what he's teaching. Leaders must have authority if they are going to lead. He's addressing the misuse of authority. The Gentiles' lording it over people was a misuse and thus an abuse of their authority. This abuse of authority wasn't to characterize the disciples' style of leadership.

What the disciples would understand from Jesus's teaching that we might miss is the pagan leader's view of humility. For a pagan, humility wasn't a virtue but a vice. They had no respect whatsoever for humility in leadership. And Jesus is serving up a strong dose of humility to those who were well aware of the pagan view. Would they get it?

Service, Not Status

Jesus continues in Matthew 20:26–28: "Instead, whoever wants to become great among you must be your servant, and whoever wants to be first must be your slave—just as the Son of Man did not come to be served, but to serve, and to give his life as a ransom for many." Combining this thought with what Jesus has just taught on humility, we find that servant leadership is about humble service. It's the kind of service that involves the giving of oneself, not taking for oneself.

Jesus uses two Greek words to express his concept of servanthood. One is *diakonos*, which in the first century referred to one who serves others voluntarily. Thus greatness in his kingdom involves being a willing servant. The other is *doulos*, which was used in the first century to refer to one who was in a servile position and had forfeited his rights. It involved giving without expecting anything in return. You served because it was your station in life; it was expected of you. Jesus uses these two terms and their first-century meanings to bring together the concepts of willingness and obligation. While we're obligated to serve him (*doulos*), we must at the same time be willing to serve him (*diakonos*). To sum it up: we *willingly obligate* ourselves to serve.

As if this wasn't enough, in verse 28 Jesus uses himself as an illustration of the kind of selfless service that he's looking for in his followers: "Just as the Son of Man did not come to be served, but to serve, and to give his life as a ransom for many." We could sum up Jesus's life and ministry with two words—*selfless service*. Jesus is calling for selfless leadership.

Focusing on Others, Not Ourselves

Next, we must consider whom servant leaders are obligated to serve selflessly. In these passages the answer for the disciples was *others*. Note Jesus's use of the personal and possessive pronouns in verse 26: "Whoever wants to become great among *you* must be *your* servant," and in verse 27: "Whoever wants to be first must be *your* slave" (emphasis added). In context Jesus is speaking to ten men who are indignant with James and John because they tried to gain an advantage over them in their pursuit of greatness. Jesus's message for them is simple. Rather than compete with one another, serve one another. We serve to benefit others, not ourselves. An example today is a little girl in Dallas, Texas, with cancer who was part of the Make a Wish Foundation. Her wish wasn't that she be healed of cancer. Her wish was that all the other kids with cancer would be healed.

Paul's Teaching on Servanthood

The Context of 1 Corinthians 9:19–23

As we looked at the context of Jesus's teaching on servanthood in Matthew 20, we must also examine the context of Paul's teaching in 1 Corinthians 9. He's teaching the Corinthian church about the believer's freedom or liberty in Christ, which apparently some of his detractors had questioned (vv. 2–3). In verse 1 he brings up his freedom in regard to his apostleship: "Am I not free? Am I not an apostle? Have I not seen Jesus our Lord? Are you not the result of my work in the Lord?" Then in verses 4–12a, he addresses other liberties, such as the right to food and drink, marriage to a believer, and the right to be supported by those to whom he ministered. He concludes in verses 12b–18 that, for the sake of the gospel, he's not using any of these rights. He didn't want to hinder anyone's response to the gospel. This served to affirm his integrity and commitment to his ministry.

The Concept of Servanthood in 1 Corinthians 9:19–23

Paul teaches the concept of servanthood in 1 Corinthians 9:19. He explains and illustrates the principle in verses 20–22a, and he repeats it again in verses 22b–23. First is the principle. Paul writes that though he is free in Christ, he has intentionally, willfully made himself a slave to those without Christ, hoping to win as many as possible to Christ (v. 19). Thus his purpose for being a servant is evangelism. Winning lost people to faith in Christ is of utmost importance to the apostle.

Then he explains how this servant concept applies, first with the Jews and then with the Gentiles and the weak. He attempts to reach Jews by becoming like them, that is, placing himself under the restrictions of the law. He then notes that as a believer, he's no longer under the law; however, he has voluntarily placed himself under it to win lost Jews to Jesus as their Messiah. In Paul's day many Jews would have been offended if he had overtly broken the law. This would have denied him the opportunity to share Christ with them. They wouldn't have listened. So Paul had a choice. He could observe the law and restrict his freedom or ignore it and risk offending those he was attempting to reach. He chose the first option at some sacrifice to his freedom in Christ.

It's much the same with the Gentiles. With the Gentiles, Paul didn't observe the restrictions of Jewish law. This doesn't mean that he lived and did as he pleased. He notes in verse 21 that he was still under law, only it was the law of God and Christ. Again this was for the purpose of winning lost Gentiles to faith in Christ.

Next, Paul concludes by repeating his concept of servanthood in verses 22–23. In essence, Paul voluntarily restricted his freedom in Christ to gain the widest possible hearing for the gospel from the lost. In the first century, Paul was writing truth that still applies in this century. The question that our evangelical churches must answer in the twenty-first century is, What are we willing to give up, change, or set aside to win lost people to faith in Christ?

The Contemporary Church

There are a number of examples of churches that have embraced a servanthood mentality. For the sake of brevity, I'll comment on three: Vineyard Community Church, Fellowship Bible Church, and Willow Creek Community Church.

Vineyard Community Church

Vineyard Community Church is in Cincinnati, Ohio. Its founding pastor was Steve Sjogren, who says that he was raised in a "loving but unchurched" family. Steve came to faith in Christ while studying abroad as a foreign exchange student.

After planting Vineyard Community Church, Steve wrote *Conspiracy of Kindness* to show how his church attempted to serve the people of Cincinnati. Specifically they chose to serve the public through a form of servant evangelism. His book presents 101 ways to share the love of Jesus in one's community with the goal of influencing and reaching them for the Savior. For example, you could anonymously wash the windows of cars parked in public places, such as a shopping mall; hold a car wash but not charge people for the service; provide free cold beverages in various parks during the summer; clean the bathrooms of local establishments, such as service stations and restaurants. Steve and his church found that people were not just "won to Christ"; they were "served to Christ."

Fellowship Bible Church

Fellowship Bible Church is located in Little Rock, Arkansas. Bill Parkinson, Bill Wellons, and later Robert Lewis, along with several families, came together with a vision to plant this church that was modeled after the fellowship Bible churches that Gene Getz started in and around Dallas, Texas. Fellowship Little Rock is a church that is committed to equipping Christians to change the world through its irresistible lifestyle and influential works of service. Its vision is summed up in the symbol I^2, which stands for the acceptance of God's challenge in Matthew 5:16 to become an *irresistible influence* to one's neighborhood, community, and the world.

The church is well-known in the Little Rock community as a loving and serving church. Like a growing number of churches early in the twenty-first century, it has a strong desire to reach out to serve its community. For example, if you were driving through the city and asked someone if he was familiar with the church, chances are good he would be. And he might comment that people from Fellowship were heavily involved in tutoring disadvantaged children in the local public schools. The church is also known in the community for a number of other service events, such as annually renting a local theme park and inviting the Little Rock Fire and Police Departments to bring their families for a day of fun and entertainment as well as a little recognition.

Willow Creek Community Church

Willow Creek Community Church, located in Barrington, Illinois, has demonstrated a servant mentality in that they have given up their weekend believers' service in deference to unbelievers. Let's face it, most of us prefer to meet as believers on the weekends, because it's much easier then. On weekends many of us have two days off from work to relax and make it to church. Worshiping on Sunday is most convenient. Willow has given up this convenience. Instead, they come back on a weeknight for their believers' service, called New Community. I believe the key to their willingness is reflected in one of their core values: lost people matter to God; therefore they should matter to us. They really believe this and are willing to do what is necessary within biblical guidelines to demonstrate it (sounds like 1 Cor. 9:19–23). Those who are familiar with Willow and what they are doing know that this is true. I suspect if more of our churches adopted the servant attitude of Willow Creek and the other churches mentioned here, we would see more people come to faith in Christ and more believers growing in Christ. As professor Howard Hendricks at Dallas Seminary would say, "May their tribe increase!"

Questions for Reflection and Discussion

1. Does the New Testament concept of servanthood characterize your church? If yes, explain how this is true, giving some specific examples. If not, why not? What would it take for it to become a serving church?
2. The author mentions several churches that illustrate a serving heart and gives several examples of how these churches serve their communities. Did you find any examples that appeal to you and might work in your church and community? If so, which ones?
3. Are you familiar with any other serving churches in addition to the ones the author mentions in this chapter? How do they demonstrate servanthood? Have any of them influenced your church? If so, how? What are they doing that has helped your church become more serving in nature?
4. Before proceeding to the next chapter, brainstorm some ways that your church might better serve your community and reach people for Christ.

9

The Thinking Church

Evaluating Church Models

A surprising number of churched people have a viewpoint about the new-model churches. Some vote for them and want to be a part of them. Others tend to vote against them or have no interest in being a part of them. And still others not only oppose them but are very critical of them. So who's right? And how can we know? These viewpoints are based on some kind of evaluation of these new churches. But is it a good one? We must determine the best way to evaluate new-model churches.

I've written this chapter to accomplish two purposes. One is to help us adopt a fair and impartial process for the evaluation of models, whether old or new. The other is to examine the arguments of many of the critics of the new models in light of my process for evaluation. This will take us back to some of their arguments in chapter 3.

A Process for Evaluating Church Models

Before I launch into the process for evaluating church models, I need to mention two things. First, the process that I will explain here can be used to evaluate any church model, older, current, and those to come. My experience is that most established churches do little formal evaluation. If they did, it could be most helpful in making needed corrections. Second, I have already presented this evaluation process in chapter 3. I review it briefly here and add to it the information gained from chapters 4–7.

As I said in chapter 3, it is the responsibility of the churches in general and their leaders in particular to police what they're doing to make sure that it is biblically and doctrinally sound. To do this, they need a process for evaluating church models that provides evaluators with a biblical-theological sieve through which they run the church's practices. This process, as developed by Philip Melanchthon in the sixteenth century, is based solidly on the Scriptures and consists of three filters.

Filter 1: The Essentials of the Faith

The first filter consists of the essentials of the faith. These essentials are the propositional truths that are both clearly taught in the Bible and are necessary for one to be considered orthodox or sound in the faith. There are at least five essentials of the faith. See them listed in the chart below.

The Essentials of the Faith

The inspiration of the Bible as the Word of God

The existence of only one true God as three coequal and coeternal persons (the Trinity)

The deity and substitutionary atonement of Christ

The bodily resurrection of Christ

The physical return of Christ

What should our response be to others in light of these core essential beliefs? The key word is unity. We pursue unity with those who agree with us on these (John 17:20–23; Eph. 4:3). But the essentials are exclusive as well as inclusive. They include people of like mind but exclude people who don't agree on these core essentials, such as those who don't base their faith on Scripture or members of a cult who reject in some way the essentials.

Filter 2: The Nonessentials

The nonessentials are those views we hold based on the Scriptures, our tradition, or both. The nonessentials aren't as clear biblically as we would like to believe, and that's why evangelicals disagree on them. What one group views as nonessential may be viewed as essential by another group. For example, one group may allow much freedom in their mode of baptism, whereas another may argue that immersion is the only correct mode. Agreement with the nonessentials doesn't affect one's faith or standing before Christ as agreement with the essentials does. The key word is *liberty*. The following chart provides us with some nonessentials.

Some Nonessentials of the Faith

Church government (polity)

Mode of baptism

Efficacy of the Lord's Supper

Role of women in the church

Presence and permanence of spiritual gifts

Time and place for the church to meet

Church practices

What should our response be to others regarding the faith nonessentials? In the essentials, we are to pursue unity and self-respect as persons created in the image of God. However, in the nonessentials we are to pursue Christian liberty. Liberty says that it is okay to take a firm position on the nonessentials, but we must recognize that we are in the realm of interpretive tradition. We must be willing to grant others their distinctive beliefs and still hold one another in high regard. Preserving the "unity of the faith" (Eph. 4:13) means treating those who differ with us on the nonessentials with love, kindness, and compassion (John 13:34–35; 15:12–14, 17). We must not falsely judge, look down on, condemn, or malign them (Rom. 14:10–13). Instead, we choose to treat one another as brothers and sisters in Christ. This is important, and we will revisit it later in this chapter when we look at the conduct of some who viciously attack new-model churches.

Filter 3: In All Things Love

The third filter affects the essentials and nonessentials. It argues that in both we treat others with love. We are to love those believers who differ on the nonessentials (John 13:34–35; 15:12–14, 17), and we are to love those who differ on the essentials (John 3:16; Rom. 5:8). We don't love what they do or teach, but we love them as fellow image bearers. However, it is imperative that we address false teaching and sinful behavior. As Jesus modeled for all, we love the individual but hate his or her sin (John 3:16).

To summarize, in the words of Philip Melanchthon: in the essentials we pursue unity and in the nonessentials liberty; in all things love.

Additional Ideas for the Process

Chapter 3 provides churches with a process for evaluating all models of church. As we examine what we're doing in our own churches as well as the new church paradigms, the process gives us a way to determine doctrinal soundness. Chapters 4–7 all address in some way how we handle or use the Scriptures in arriving at our view of the church.

A Biblical Hermeneutic

Chapter 4 addresses our need for a solid, biblical hermeneutic, for interpreting not only Scripture in general but the passages that address how we do church in particular. The process that I've presented in chapter 3 and summarized above is based on and entirely dependent on how well we handle or interpret Scripture. Most of us will agree that what we believe in terms of church models must be based on or at least not contradict the clear teaching of the Bible. However, if we've misinterpreted the Scriptures on any of these issues, we will mistakenly and unfairly criticize or praise the models we assess (and I see much of this).

A Biblical Theology of Change

Chapter 5 provides the church with a theology of change that consists of three elements: function, form, and freedom. Again this theology of change is based on the Scriptures and helps us determine where the

Bible does and doesn't address change issues, and where each church has the freedom to make its own decisions regarding its ministries. The functions are those eternal, unchanging precepts or mandates that are based squarely on the clear teaching of the Bible. They are teaching, fellowship, worship, evangelism, and service (Acts 2:42–47).

The forms are the temporal, changing practices that are based on culture, not Scripture. They are methods from which all churches are free to choose to accomplish their functions. That they aren't mandated by Scripture means that God has given his churches the freedom to choose these as necessary. We must not attempt to hand down mandates or legislate in this area of freedom unless we can clearly show that some Scripture has been violated.

A Biblical Theology of Culture

In chapter 6 I provide the church with a theology of culture. It is based on the Bible and helps us understand how the culture in which we live affects what we practice in our churches. A person's view of culture will highly affect how he or she assesses both new- and old-model churches. Some equate culture with Satan's world system and conclude that anything that has to do with or reflects in some way one's culture is bad. Scripture, however, teaches that culture is neutral. It's a vehicle that can be used for good or bad. It's not an end in itself; rather it is a means or vehicle to an end (see, for example, Romans 14:14, having to do with food, and James 3:9–12, dealing with language).

A Biblical Definition of the Church

In chapter 7 I attempt to provide you with a working, biblical definition of the local church. I define a local church as an indispensable gathering of professing believers in Christ who, under leadership, are organized to pursue its mission (the Great Commission) through its functions (biblical teaching, worship, fellowship, evangelism, and service) to accomplish its purpose (the glory of God). In addressing different model churches we need a definition of the church in hand. How do we know if a new- or old-model church really qualifies biblically as a church? Does a new model contain these elements? Does an older, inward focused model that views itself strictly as one small, happy family, taking care of its people through a chaplain, qualify as a church?

Here is where I walk on questionable ground, because many good, biblical theologians provide different definitions (Luther and Calvin as well as many today), and the Bible doesn't give us a precise definition to direct us. Instead, you must look at the different biblical characteristics and arrive at a definition based on them. I would categorize this as a "necessary nonessential." While a definition of the church is necessary to evaluate the different models, we must be careful not to say that our definition is the biblical definition or the only correct one. Our response must be guarded in that we don't condemn others because their definition doesn't precisely align with ours. We can debate the differences, but we must do so in a spirit of love for one another that seeks the truth for the sake of the church.

Key Arguments of the Critics of New-Model Churches

Now that we have a process in place for evaluating new- or old-model churches, I would like to examine some of the arguments that are currently being used against new-model churches in particular. Before I do so, I must present several assumptions that undergird this discussion.

1. We would be silly not to believe that some of these views are true of some churches out there. However, arguments that attempt to characterize all new-model churches as wrong or bad are spurious at best and sinful at worst.
2. Many of the arguments that are leveled against new-model churches can also be leveled at some old-model and current-model churches.
3. If you enter this discussion with a closed mind, it is likely that you will not benefit from it as you should. Actually, the following may upset you, and you will put this book down in anger before you finish the chapter. I ask you at least to give this section a fair hearing.

I've divided the rest of this chapter into two parts. In the first I examine and respond to the general arguments against new-model churches that I presented in chapter 3. In the second I present some general issues that face the critics of new-model churches.

General Arguments

Critics present a number of arguments against new-model churches and the changes they've introduced to the church. I believe that most of them fall under the six categories presented in chapter 3. Below I'll present the argument, respond to it, and issue a challenge to the churches.

The Proclamation of Scripture

The first argument deals with how new-paradigm churches handle Scripture.

The argument: Many critics argue that the new models in general and seeker churches in particular downplay the preaching and teaching of God's Word. I consider this a most serious accusation, but it is likely true of some new-model churches. As one who is involved in theological education at the seminary level, I've observed that a growing number of new-model pastors and church planters have little if any biblical and theological training. There are several reasons for this. First, there is such a dearth of leadership out there that many churches, denominations, missions, and other organizations aren't requiring theological preparation. Another is that those leading larger "successful" churches see a huge discrepancy between what they're doing in ministry and what seminaries are preparing their students to do in ministry. One person observes that seminaries prepare students to preach, while the corporate world trains them to lead.

However, to say that new-model churches downplay the preaching and teaching of God's Word is a sweeping generalization. That's certainly not true of all these churches. All one has to do to dispel this argument is to produce a new-model church that does preach and teach the Bible well, and I can provide you with more than one. In some cases the critics will attack a particular church. When they do this, it becomes a matter of opinion or one's judgment based not on firsthand experience but on another critic's assessment (I'll address this below). A church that many have accused of such preaching and teaching is Willow Creek Community Church where Bill Hybels is the pastor and lead teacher. Unlike some of its critics, I've actually attended Willow's seeker services and believers services (New Community) and found them to be not only biblically sound but spiritually challenging.

The critics continue their argument with the accusation that preaching in these new churches is topical and not expositional, that the sermons are essentially "feel good" practical messages that are a soft sell of Christianity. Rick Warren, the pastor of Saddleback Church in California, faced these criticisms early in his ministry as he addressed certain topics from the Bible that his audience struggled with, such as various addictions and fears.

I'll address two issues raised here. Critics must be more careful about their use of the terms *topical* and *expositional* when used of preaching. What some mean is that the preaching in the new churches is topical as done in liberal churches, where often the message is on a topic that may not even be found in the Bible or the preacher ignores the Bible. Again this may be true of a handful of new-model churches but by no means all.

Many of us who teach preaching at a seminary level divide expository preaching into several areas, all of which are based on preaching the Bible. Three such areas are book exposition, biographical exposition, and topical exposition. Book exposition involves preaching through various books of the Bible. Biographical exposition is preaching the lives of biblical characters, based on what the text says about them. And topical exposition is preaching on various topics addressed in Scripture, for example, what the Bible says about worry, money, abortion, capital punishment, and such theological topics as angels, salvation, sin, the Trinity, and so on. Thus it is okay to preach a topical sermon, as long as it is topical exposition. How else might we preach systematic or biblical theology or some other subject of the Bible?

Critics must be careful of the terminology they use when it comes to preaching and teaching the Bible. The accusation that sermons are "feel good," practical messages that do a soft sell of Christianity is somewhat nebulous. The natural response is, "Says who?" This is strictly a judgment call on someone's part. What may be "feel good" and a "soft sell" to one person isn't to another. I believe that many of these new pastors are reacting to what they believe are long, boring, pointless sermons preached in older model churches. They want their audiences to see how the Bible is practical and applies to our lives in the twenty-first century as well as the first century. However, the critics may be right about some of the new churches—likely a small number—who go overboard in the wrong direction.

The challenge: Those who preach in new-model or older model churches must make sure they're preaching expository sermons. Do they allow the text or their personal opinions on a particular topic to direct their messages? The Bible must be central to all preaching and teaching in the church. Those who preach in newer model churches need to step back periodically and ask if they've gone too far in attempting to attract lost, unchurched people. This might be, for example, when they use a text of the Bible to preach a topic that the passage isn't addressing or a topic that is secondary to the teaching of the text. I recently heard a message on stress that used the Martha and Mary text in Luke 10:38–42. The problem is this section is teaching the importance of spiritual priorities—we must give the Lord and his Word priority in our lives, even over loving service.

Another problem is using a biblical text as a launching pad to address some other topic that the individual text or maybe even the entire Bible doesn't address. This conveys the idea that because the preacher cited or even read a biblical text, the entire message is based on the Bible when it isn't. This can be true of older model churches as well as some newer models.

The Focus of Sunday Morning Worship

Some critics find fault with what certain new-model churches do in their prime-time Sunday morning worship services in general and what seeker model churches do in particular—they focus on unchurched, lost people.

The argument: My experience is that many critics don't understand the seeker concept. They assume that the Sunday morning worship time at a seeker church is a normal worship service for believers and judge what takes place accordingly. Obviously this is unfair to the seeker church and is a straw man argument logically.

Critics who do understand the seeker model argue that Sunday morning should be a time of edification for the church, not of evangelism for the lost. I've already addressed this accusation in chapter 8.

The Seeker Concept

At this point it's imperative that I pause and discuss the seeker concept as practiced by Willow Creek Community Church. I will explain the concept and Willow Creek's seeker service and show how the church exemplifies Christ's and Paul's teachings on servanthood.

I appeal to you, the reader, to hold your criticism of this church model and try to read about it with an open mind. Try to see how this church is following Christ's directive to be a servant to other churches and to unbelievers as they seek to win people to Christ.

A Much Maligned Concept

Willow Creek Community Church is one of the most vilified churches of the new church models. If you question this, then type in the name on Google and see what comes up. This criticism focuses primarily on their seeker approach in general and their seeker service on Sunday mornings in particular. However, what I've discovered is that few critics understand Willow's approach to reaching seekers. For example, several years ago a well-known Bible teacher with a large following criticized Willow in *Leadership Journal* for the lack of biblical depth in their Sunday morning service. He assumed Willow's Sunday morning service was for believers. In other words, he was operating under a false assumption. He hadn't done his homework and had unknowingly created a straw man argument. In a later article in the same journal, he corrected his earlier statement but was still critical of Willow, because he felt that Willow's Sunday morning service should be for believers and not seekers.

I was amazed by this criticism because Scripture grants a church much flexibility as to when it worships, and it directs us not to judge others in these matters (Rom. 14:1–13). In his criticism of Willow, this Bible teacher had clearly violated this injunction. And unfortunately, this critic's following holds the same views. I'm troubled by the extremes some will go to in criticizing the seeker movement.

Clarity of the Concept

I believe that much of the criticism of Willow Creek Community Church and its emphasis on reaching lost people through a seeker service comes from a misunderstanding of the seeker concept and what Scripture says on this topic. The critics of this approach that I have spoken with can rarely articulate clearly what Willow's approach is. And unfortunately, most have simply read what another critic has written about the concept rather than doing their own investigation.

First, let's look at the concept. Bill and Lynne Hybels have written *Rediscovering Church* in which they present the story and vision of Willow Creek Church.[1] In chapter 11 on mission and strategy, they clearly articulate the seeker concept that is step 4 in their seven-step strategy. Essentially, they have designed their weekend services specifically for the unchurched lost person. This is so the Willow congregation can bring their lost friends to a service specifically designed for them from start to finish.

I see several advantages to this approach. First, it encourages and can potentially involve the entire congregation in evangelism, which simply doesn't happen in most churches around the world. (Far too many congregations believe that it is the pastor's job not only to do the work of the ministry for them but to win people to Christ.)

A second advantage is that it allows the church to focus what they're doing. Willow has separate services for believers, meeting on separate nights during the week. Thus their approach allows them to focus specifically on the purpose and nature of each meeting. One service is designed for lost people, and the other for saved people.

I can recall my early days as a pastor when I attempted to do both on a Sunday morning. I must admit that in the Bible or teaching churches I pastored, evangelism always got the short end of the stick. It became an "add on." At the end of a service designed strictly for believers, I would give a brief explanation of the gospel along with an invitation to accept Christ. Few responded.

Objections to the Concept

What does Scripture say about the seeker concept? Does the Bible speak against such an approach? The answer is an unequivocal no!

Here are some of the objections I've heard to the seeker approach. One is that, according to Romans 3:11, people are not able to seek after God. "There is no one who understands, no one who seeks (*ekzateo*) God." This is important, because it would potentially undermine the theology of the seeker movement. However, in Acts 17:26–27 Paul says to a group of Epicurean and Stoic philosophers: "From one man he made every nation of men, that they should inhabit the whole earth; and he determined the times set for them and the exact places where they should live. God did this so that men would *seek* (*zateo*) him and perhaps reach out for him and find him, though he is not far from each one of us." Note that here Paul uses a slight variation (*zateo*) of the Greek word that was used in the Romans passage. We must not explain this away by assuming it's a different Greek word or a bad translation.

There appears to be a contradiction between the two verses. In Romans 3:11 Paul is teaching that lost people in and of themselves can't seek or even come to God. The implication in Acts 17:26–27 is that they can. I believe the difference is the convicting (John 16:8–11) and regenerating work (Titus 3:5) of the Holy Spirit in an unbeliever's life. When the Holy Spirit begins this work in the lives of God's elect, he enables lost people to seek after God and thus come to faith. In addition, we have several examples of seekers in the Bible—Zacchaeus, Cornelius and his relatives and close friends, the Ethiopian eunuch, Lydia, and others who obviously were seeking God.

Another objection to the seeker approach is that the meetings in the church facility should be only for believers, to train them in the Bible so that they can go out into the world and win people to Christ. This is merely an opinion. Those who argue this way don't cite any biblical support. The reason is there is none.

A third objection is that the church (believers) should meet on the weekends because the early church met on the first day of the week. Scripture does say that some churches met on the first day of the week. If the meeting that took place in Acts 20:7 was a church meeting, and I think it was, then the church at Troas met on Sunday, the first day of the week, perhaps in the evening. Also Paul tells the Corinthians to set aside funds on the first day of the week, which may indicate that they met on that day.

We should note, however, that these passages aren't binding on the church. Both are descriptive and not prescriptive, a concept that I covered in chapter 4. In addition, Luke observes that the Jerusalem church met every day (Acts 2:46). So which church are we to follow? John states in Revelation 1:10 that he was in the Spirit on the Lord's Day. Many interpret this as Sunday. However, there is no evidence for this. Finally, Romans 14:1–13 is very clear and teaches that it is up to the individual believer as to when he or she observes special days of worship: "One man considers one day more sacred than another; another man considers every day alike. Each one should be fully convinced in his own mind" (v. 5). What's important isn't *when* a church meets but *what takes place* when it meets. Furthermore, Paul clearly warns those who would judge others in these matters not to do so (vv. 10–13).

Recently I shared all this with an avid Willow Creek critic. His response was to agree reluctantly, but his closing remark was he still didn't like it. This was an emotional response that causes me to wonder what is really taking place in this man's life. What he should have said is that all this is a matter of preference, not right or wrong, and that he has a preference for a different approach but wished Willow Creek well in their approach. That would be a more biblical response.

The challenge: Having said all this in favor of the seeker model, I do believe that seeker churches aren't without their difficulties. What I've observed from a church-starting perspective is that seeker churches are difficult to plant. I worked with one such church where the preaching pastor put so much time and energy into the Sunday morning seeker service that he had nothing left for the midweek believers service, what Willow and others who follow the Willow model refer to as New Community. Eventually the church's core believers began to atrophy spiritually and drifted away to other churches, looking for spiritual food. Therefore, I advise anyone starting a seeker church to use two teams. One is responsible for the Sunday morning seeker service, and the other is responsible for New Community.

Another concern that I have is how long people will respond to the seeker approach. It's a model, and all models have a shelf life. Certainly the Boomer generation has responded well. However, a growing number of us have observed that the younger, postmodern generations (even those attending seeker model churches) prefer a different approach that involves ministry primarily through authentic small groups. Should this continue, my concern is whether seeker churches will make the adjustments necessary to reach this younger generation or go the way of other models that have reached the end of their shelf life.

The Church and Evangelism

Many critics agree that the new-model churches preach the gospel, but they challenge their motives and results.

The argument: Some critics argue that the new-model churches soft-pedal the gospel to keep people in the pews and that their gospel fails to move people out of the world and into God's kingdom. In essence they're impugning the motives of these churches. It's most difficult to judge what someone's true motivation is unless he or she articulates it. Perhaps we could argue that a person's behavior or beliefs reveal his or her motives (Matt. 7:16). However, we must tread softly here as this is difficult to judge, and we all prove to be hypocrites at times. Does the gospel in new-model churches fail to move people out of the world and into God's kingdom? It depends on your definition of the gospel. Some believe that the gospel includes a commitment before salvation to let Jesus control one's life after salvation. This is the lordship salvation view. Others correctly point out that this view mixes salvation with sanctification and adds works to the gospel, which is a false gospel (Gal. 1:6–10). They argue that salvation is by grace through faith in Christ alone (Eph. 2:8–9), and for a person to be saved, he or she doesn't have to agree to behave a certain way after salvation. I've noted that some who believe in lordship salvation tend to be critical of the gospel of grace that is often heard in new-model churches.

The challenge: It's most likely that some new-model churches are preaching the gospel for the wrong reasons. This isn't new in the twenty-first century. Much the same thing happened in the church at Philippi (Phil. 1:12–18) in the first century, but Paul rejoices that the gospel is preached nevertheless.

New-paradigm churches should regularly assess their motives for what they do. I believe there are some churches out there that fail to challenge their converts to make Christ Lord of their lives after they are saved (lordship isn't necessary for salvation but is vital to one's sanctification). This is Paul's message in Romans 6–8. I challenge these churches to examine their converts, looking for fruit in their lives. How do they know these people are believers? Is there fruit? If not, why not? What might this say about their ministries to these people?

The Church's Methodology

Some critics find fault with how the church does what it does, its philosophy of ministry.

The argument: Many critics believe that the church must not use what they refer to as secular means to reach people, whether saved or lost. Secular means are what some would call marketing devices and include such tools as film clips, skits, comedy, pyrotechnics, light shows, smoke machines, and an overindulgence in contemporary music. Mars Hill Church in Seattle, like many churches today, uses a rock band to play in its worship services. Not only does the band play contemporary music, but some of the musicians playing in this emerging church's services have long hair and a few have tattoos.

The problem with this criticism is that these critics fail to have a biblical view of culture. In my discussion of this topic in chapter 6, we learned that culture is a vehicle that may be used for good or bad. Thus the way a church uses these vehicles determines whether they are good or bad.

It is possible, of course, for a church to misuse these tools. An example would be if they use them for the wrong reasons, such as merely to entertain people. And this really doesn't make sense. Why would a church go to all the expense and trouble merely to entertain people? I know of few new-model pastors who aren't using these means to merit a hearing and win people to Christ.

Further, I would argue that if using a smoke machine or putting on a skit in some way promotes the proclamation of the gospel, then why not use them? These vehicles aren't wrong in themselves and can easily enhance the presentation of the gospel. If an unbeliever observes these means and is attracted to the ministry because he or she feels that the church has finally come into the twenty-first century, that's a good thing. However, if these means are distracting and turning lost people away from the gospel, the church needs to look for other means to convey the message.

The critics must realize that criticism of forms, similar to what they are voicing today, has been voiced through the years. An example is criticism of the organ. Initially people frowned on the use of the organ in church. And while it is true that there was a time when you found guitars and drums mostly in bars or rock bands, that doesn't mean that a church can't use them today. The same argument could be used against the piano, but simply because several famous gay men play the piano well, it doesn't mean we can't use it in the church. Perhaps the classic that I came across recently is criticism of the use of coffee. Writing in the *Clapham Commentary*, Mike Metzger observes:

> In the early 1600s, coffee first reached Europe. The first coffeehouse opened in Italy in 1654. But not everyone consumed the drink, including many religious people who viewed it as immoral. In 1674, an English movement—called the Women's Petition Against Coffee—declared: "Coffee leads men to trifle away their time, scald their chops, and spend their money." Fast forward: Today, most churches serve coffee after every service and many are building coffeehouses on their premises.[2]

One other issue here is some critics' use of the term *secular*. They would be better off staying away from such a term, because this is a Roman Catholic concept. It was developed and used by the Catholic Church back in the Middle Ages. The church viewed everything that took place within the walls of the church as sacred and everything that took place outside the walls as secular. It totally misses the point that the church is people and the place where it meets is its facility. Further, one doesn't have to think about this for long to realize that often what takes place within the walls of the church isn't always good, and what takes place outside may be good.

The challenge: Both new- and old-model churches must regularly evaluate their methodology or ministry forms. New-model churches must determine if their forms are promoting or hindering the gospel, and consider the reason for using a particular form. Often, because these churches are new, they're more in touch with what people are responding to.

Old-model churches must also evaluate their methodology. Many tend to continue to use methods that have long since lost their edge in delivering God-honoring ministry. A ministry's shelf life is limited to a certain amount of time.

The Motives for the Church's Ministry

Many if not most critics attack the new-model churches for their motives.

The argument: In some way each of the arguments above questions a church's motives. I've noted this in several of them. A church's motives address why it does what it does. At issue here is whether anyone's motives are 100 percent pure. My experience is that all our motives are mixed to some degree, because God didn't see fit to eradicate our flesh (see Rom. 7:14). Regardless, the critics believe that the new-model churches do what they do for all the wrong motives, such as wanting to draw large numbers to fill their pews, soft-pedaling the gospel to keep people in the pews, and appealing to the desires or flesh of unregenerate persons.

The challenge: All model churches must be aware of their motives or why they do what they do. Paul sets the example for this in 1 Thessalonians 2:1–10. For him to comment on his motives means that he's aware of them. I would challenge all of us, critics included, to set aside some time to list our major ministry goals. Once we have these down, we would be wise to consider the reasons for our pursuing each one. Undoubtedly, we'll find that some of our motives are mixed, and this will be the time to address this problem.

The Church's Goals

Some critics question the goals of new-model churches.

The argument: These critics argue that the new-model church's goal is to bring lots of people into the church and keep them interested so they will come back. So what's wrong with that? To make my point, let's consider the opposite. Should the goal of these churches be to bring few people in and bore them to tears so they will not come back? Does this sound familiar? Unfortunately, it's the description of far too many of today's evangelical churches that are dying in great numbers all across America as well as abroad.

At the same time, many new-model churches have caught a fresh commitment to Christ's Great Commission as their megagoal and want to see people saved as well as sanctified. Their goal is the Great Commission. This is the case with Mars Hill Church in Seattle. Their mission is to get the attention of people who visit their services so they will come back. How else will they lead them to Christ and disciple them?

If some new-model churches are to be criticized for anything, it might be for failing to encourage spiritual depth after people get saved. But this is by no means true of all of the new-model churches, as some critics would have us believe.

The challenge: Both older and newer model churches would do well to look at their goals. What are their goals—spoken or unspoken? Is their primary goal the Great Commission? If not, why not?

A Critique of the Critics

As we saw in chapter 3, the church in general and leaders in particular must police their ministries, which is a form of contending for the faith. To some degree they have to play the role of the critic. However, playing the role of the critic is the easy part. Anyone can throw darts. The hard part is doing some housekeeping of our own. As I've read books by some critics and spoken with others, I find that all critics—myself included—need to take a look at our own ministry. We need to take stock of what we're doing or how we're doing what we're doing (our methods and motives).

Here are several observations that amount to a critique of the critics.

Sweeping Generalizations

Critics make sweeping generalizations. I've made this observation already. However, it bears repeating. Some criticism is true of any model—old or new. So to a certain degree we all may be pronounced guilty as charged. However, critics, in their broad generalizations, leave you thinking that all new-model churches are guilty as charged. All anyone has to do is to find one example to prove this wrong, and I can cite numerous examples demonstrating that the broad generalizations are not true of all new-model churches.

Questionable Sources

Many critics base their information on secondhand and thirdhand sources. This is questionable at best and most unfair at worst. Everyday life teaches us that this is wrong. How many times have we heard something from some person about another only to learn later that the information was wrong? When I hear a complaint against a church, for example, I make a point of asking the critic when he or she visited that church. The answer every time is that the person hasn't. My follow-up question is, Where did you get your information? The answer is from someone who is a critic of the church (who, by the way, is likely to base his criticism on second- and thirdhand sources as well!).

The obvious solution here is to get our information firsthand. We need to go to the original source. In some cases it's as easy as making an appointment with a pastor or leader. In other cases we may need to read a book by the pastor or leader in question. If we are unable to verify the information from a firsthand source, then we must desist from saying anything at all, much less resorting to criticism. I cited earlier in this book a well-known Bible teacher who has a large following. He seriously criticized Willow Creek Community Church regarding its seeker service. When I read his comments, I realized that he didn't understand the seeker approach. He assumed that Willow's Sunday morning service is a service for believers. The problem is that many of his followers have taken up the same cause based on the same wrong information. This is most unfortunate and wrong.

Logical Fallacies

Critics are guilty of logical fallacies. The example that I just cited of the well-known Bible teacher is an example of what I refer to as a straw-man argument—a logical fallacy. This is when a person creates or describes a situation that isn't true to begin with but that he or she thinks is true (in this case it happened because the person hadn't done his homework), and then the critic tears apart the situation. This is unfair representation.

Sweeping generalizations are also logical fallacies. Critics are mistaken when they intimate that everyone in a certain group believes a certain way. We must be careful when making such absolute statements. All one has to do is find one exception to prove the inadequacy of our assertions.

Critics also make false assumptions. There are certain practices that they have always viewed as incorrect, even if they're mistaken. Thus, when they see someone promoting one of these practices, they attack. An example here is marketing. Many critics of the new-paradigm churches attack the use of marketing practices. What the critics fail to realize is that every church markets its ministries. The essence of marketing is communication. You communicate who you are and why you're in a community so people are aware of your presence. How can guests visit your church if they don't know that it's in the community?

Another logical fallacy is believing the end justifies the means. For example, if a pastor and a church are (in the critic's opinion) promoting false doctrine or entertainment in the church, then it's okay to do whatever is necessary to deal with them. We can be ugly and mean-spirited and accept what others are saying about them without verifying the source or researching this on our own. If you are involved in this kind of criticism, you must stop and think about what you are doing and saying. Don't get so caught up in your crusade to correct the church's so-called errors that you resort to such practices. It's never biblical to do what is bad and wrong to accomplish what is good and right. The end never justifies the means.

Being Close-Minded

Critics are often close-minded. I once interacted by email with a critic of the seeker model church. I found that like so many he didn't really understand the model, so I took time out to explain it to him. Then I showed him from the Scriptures how churches have the freedom to meet on any day of the week and not just Sunday (Rom. 14:5–6). He really had no response. Scripture is clear on this. When all was said and done, someone asked him what he thought. His answer was that it really didn't matter; churches should have their believers services on Sunday. In other words, don't confuse me with the facts; my mind is already made up.

Critics must realize that they make decisions on at least two levels. One is the intellectual (thinking or reasoning) level and the other is the emotional level. The former is an open-minded response and the latter is close-minded. All of us have changed our minds on some issue. And it's likely that what led to such a change was discussion and thought at the intellectual level, not the emotional level. Change happens at the latter when something else happens to the person at an emotional, not an intellectual, level. We must always be open to rethinking an issue. Maybe we didn't have all the facts or enough information the first time we addressed it. Maybe it's time to revisit it, especially if it's a nonessential (see the discussion above and in chapter 3). Note Isaiah's admonition to Israel: "'Come now, let us reason together,' says the LORD" (Isa. 1:18). If we are not willing to do this, we must wonder why.

You may be thinking, *This is okay for the nonessentials but not the essentials.* Over the years I've discovered that beliefs that are accepted without some examination are often the first beliefs to be jettisoned when challenged. (We see this happen far too frequently to our youth who grow up in our churches and then go off to college.) On the other hand, the examination or reexamination of what we believe often confirms and solidifies our beliefs for the right reasons.

Unloving Criticism

Critics can be most unloving in their criticism. When I read books by critics or look at their websites or read letters to pastors, the writer usually describes new-model churches and what they do with terms such as "feel good," "warm fuzzies," "taking their cues from the world," "slick," "entertaining," "soft sell," "sacrificing substance for style," "catering to fleshly desires," "salesmanship," "just like a rock concert," "like attending a concert where they have wet T-shirt contests," and so forth. Believers' use of such emotion-laden, derogatory terms to describe the work of brothers and sisters in Christ is really disappointing at best and shameful at worst. The criticism is not only mean-spirited but makes me wonder what is really going on for these critics to feel they need to use such negative, offensive terms. They don't sound like loving Christians who are concerned about their brothers and sisters in Christ, as some profess. Does contending for the faith justify the use of this kind of inflammatory language? Not according to the Bible: "Instead, speaking the truth [biblical teaching, according to verse 15], in love, we will in all things grow up into him who is the Head, that is, Christ" (Eph. 4:15). And again, in the same context: "Do not let any unwholesome talk come out of your mouths, but only what is helpful for building others up according to their needs, that it may benefit those who listen" (v. 29).

Assessing True Motives

Critics need to assess their true motives. They need to pause in contending for the faith and ask themselves before God why they are doing what they're doing and saying what they're saying, especially if it's something ugly and derogatory about a brother in Christ. In itself, this behavior should be a red flag. I sense that deep down below the surface much anger lies.

Many would say that it's okay to be angry, and they're angry at those who have departed from the faith. They believe that theirs is a righteous indignation, along the lines of Ephesians 4:26: "In your anger do not sin: Do not let the sun go down while you are still angry." This verse does teach that there is good anger as well as bad anger. However, the critics need to cite the whole verse and be committed to resolving their anger issues quickly. Often I've found that people don't do this. Usually they are slow to resolve the issues that cause their anger, if they attempt to resolve them at all.

I sense that something else is going on. Many people are angry in general. I suspect that this anger comes from other sources and situations and has been directed at other brothers and sisters, rather than directed to the real source.

Another motive for criticism may be a fear of change. We should acknowledge that we all struggle with change at some point. We can handle only so much of it—some more than others. And we reach a point where we may lash out at those who are pushing our change buttons.

Many people are critical because they desire to maintain their preferences or traditions. As I discussed in an earlier chapter, there's nothing wrong with having preferences and holding to traditions unless they get in the way of Scripture. But we must ask, Who are we to insist on our preferences and traditions? Instead, true servanthood means we must be willing to defer to what is best for the whole church or for unbelievers, which often isn't what we prefer. Paul says in Philippians 2:3–4: "Do nothing out of selfish ambition or vain conceit, but in humility consider others better than yourselves. Each of you should look not only to your own interests, but also to the interests of others." He follows this with the illustration in verses 5–8 of how the Savior did this very thing for us through his incarnation and death.

Assessing One's General Outlook

Critics need to assess their general, overall outlook on life. Are they optimists or pessimists? I find that criticism rolls naturally and quickly off the lips of most pessimists. They believe that the glass is half empty and that Murphy's Law is true: If anything can go wrong, it will go wrong! And some defend this by saying that they're realists. However, Scripture defers to optimism and those for whom the glass is half full. And Murphy was wrong. Some translations render the beginning of Proverbs 23:7: "As a man thinks in his heart, so is he." This may not be the best translation, but most agree that it's true. And those who are critical in their thinking are critical people in life.

So how should we think? Should we contend for the faith? Of course we should, but note that Paul says, "Finally, brothers, whatever is true, whatever is noble, whatever is right, whatever is pure, whatever is lovely, whatever is admirable—if anything is excellent or praiseworthy—think about such things" (Phil. 4:8). These are positives, not negatives! How could Christians be anything but optimists? Romans 8:28 says that God works all things out—the bad as well as the good—for our good. Some might think that I'm being a little hard on pessimists, but they must understand that I'm a reformed pessimist, and in this paragraph I'm preaching to myself as well as to other Christian pessimists.

Grumbling and Complaining

Critics need to examine carefully how they respond to what they think is wrong. Scripture teaches that there's a way *not* to respond to what we might think is error. My experience has been that critics do lots of complaining, arguing, grumbling, and murmuring, whether they're upset with some new-model church or their own church (especially if their own church is moving toward becoming a new-model church). I've seen this happen so often over the years that my patience is beginning to wear thin with these people. This behavior is totally unbiblical and needs to be addressed. To such Paul commands, "Do everything without complaining or arguing, so that you may become blameless and pure" (Phil. 2:14–15). Peter commands, "Offer hospitality to one another without grumbling" (1 Pet. 4:9). And finally, Paul warns, "And do not grumble, as some of them did—and were killed by the destroying angel" (1 Cor. 10:10). In this context Paul is referring to Israel and their failures, including much grumbling, while attempting to go into the Promised Land. But he issues a dire warning to those who opt for grumbling. Paul is using Israel as an example of what could happen to the Corinthian believers if they insisted on grumbling. And this would certainly apply to today's churches.

I've noted that pastors and other church leaders tend to laugh these people off and say, "Oh, that's just the way old Fred (or Mary) is. Don't take him (or her) too seriously." If you really love Fred and Mary, you won't respond this way for their sake. Scripture teaches that there is a correct way to respond to what one believes is wrong, and it doesn't include grumbling. When we hear people in our churches responding this way, I believe that the general tenor of Scripture tells us to go to these people and address their behavior with them. If they don't repent, then they should be disciplined (see Matthew 5:23–24 and 18:15–20 for how to handle problems with others, and Galatians 2:11–14 for how Paul confronted Peter about his sin).

At the same time, we must implement in our churches a biblical grievance process. We need to have a process in place that allows people to address problems in the church (see chapter 2 in my book *Advanced Strategic Planning*, second edition, for such a process). Simply to tell people not to complain is not enough. Some people have legitimate grievances and must have a way to deal with them. Most often this involves going to the person who is responsible for the area they are having a problem with and expressing their concern without complaining and murmuring.

For those who are murmuring and complaining about new-model churches other than their own, this is more difficult. Perhaps in some situations they can actually address these churches in some way to air their grievances. However, when they can't do this, which is most often the case, out of Christian love critics would be wise to pray for new-model churches rather than complain about them.

Define Terms

Critics need to define their terms. Critics offer a long list of practices they're against. The example I've used before is marketing. My question is, What do they mean when they use this term? There is a real need to define these vague terms. While I may initially argue with you over marketing in the church, once you define the term, at least we know that we are or aren't talking about the same thing. I may agree with your argument against marketing when I hear your definition of it.

When we define the terms we use, it helps those who are listening to understand what we're talking about. It also gives them the opportunity to challenge our definition and thinking on the concept.

Another issue is entertainment. Most critics are against entertainment in the church. But what do they mean by *entertainment*? I've never heard them define it. All they know is that they're against it. Exactly what is it? Are the critics finding fault with anything to do with enjoying oneself in church? Do we really not want this to take place? Is it wrong to have fun at church? What does the Bible teach about entertainment, if anything? If we're against entertainment in the church, then what is the alternative? Can some go too far? I suspect so, but where is the line, and who determines where you draw that line?

Critics may be concerned about churches that primarily seek to give visitors or seekers a pleasant experience without addressing the aspects of sin in their life. If this is the case, they have a valid concern.

Mishandling Scripture

Many critics mishandle and violate Scripture, doing the very thing that they accuse others of doing. They fail to properly interpret the Bible. This is a failure to correctly handle the word of truth (2 Tim. 2:15). This may involve taking passages out of their context.

In addition to violating context, some don't understand what the Bible teaches about a concept and wind up criticizing God-inspired, biblical teaching. I read some material by a missionary in which he was criticizing the emphasis on addressing people's needs, an emphasis that you often hear in newer model churches. He felt that this was unbiblical. However, he failed to realize that the Bible provides us with a theology of needs (Acts 2:45; 2 Cor. 8:14; 9:12; Eph. 4:29; Phil. 4:19).

Critics may violate clear biblical teaching. For example, in Hebrews 13:17 the writer clearly instructs congregants to obey their leaders and submit to their authority. My experience has been that some critics ignore this passage and work in unison to oppose and even in some cases to depose their leaders. Once critics have gone through the proper channels, such as a biblical grievance process, if the leadership disagrees with their position, the proper biblical response is to back off and submit to the leadership. If they feel they can't comply, then it's time to move on.

Consider Other Alternatives

Critics need to consider alternative responses to the new-model churches. I've already indicated above that mean-spirited criticism of one's brothers in Christ as well as constant complaining and murmuring can be dangerous to one's health (see 1 Cor. 10:10). I believe that critics of churches need to think of some alternative responses. For those whose own churches are moving in a new direction, one response is to find another church where they agree with what is taking place. In the 1960s there was a cigarette commercial (sorry about the analogy) where the tagline said, "I'd rather fight than switch [brands]!" A good alternative for critics of their church's ministry is this tagline: "I'd rather switch (churches) than fight!" If you're so unhappy with your church, why don't you find a church that meets your standards for ministry? Wouldn't you be far happier? If the answer is you can't find such a church, then maybe this says something about you and your standards. Others have responded, "But we were here first." So what does that mean? Are you saying this is your church? Christ would strongly differ with you about that. In Matthew 16:18 he says it's his church, not yours.

For those who are concerned about new-model churches other than their own, at the very least they could pray for these churches rather than criticize them. When possible, they should enter into dialogue with them. When this isn't possible, they should make sure they've got all the facts and aren't relying on what someone else says. If they still hold to their opinion, they should commit the churches to God and let him take care of correcting them.

Questions for Discussion and Reflection

1. Do you agree that the church needs to police itself in terms of its doctrine and practices? Why or why not?
2. Do you believe that the author has provided the church with a good process with which to police itself? Why or why not? Do you find the information in chapters 4–7 helpful in this process? Why or why not?

3. Do you believe that the author has grasped the major arguments used by most critics of the newer church models? If not, what has he missed? Do you feel that he's treated these arguments fairly? If not, why not?

4. Are you familiar with Willow Creek Community Church? If so, are you indifferent toward, a critic of, or sympathetic with the seeker movement in general and Willow Creek in particular? Why? Does this influence your reading of this book? How?

5. If you are a critic of the seeker movement, have you ever attended Willow Creek or a seeker-styled church? If not, from where are you getting your information about Willow Creek and the movement? If from another critic, how do you know that person is correct? Would it not be better for you to either attend the church or read one of Bill Hybels's books that explains the approach from Willow's perspective? Why or why not?

6. If you're a critic of Willow Creek and the seeker movement, did you understand the seeker concept before reading this chapter? If not, do you understand it now? Regardless, do you agree or still disagree with it? If so, what are the grounds for your disagreement? Do you find that the grounds are mostly emotional and you find it difficult to mount a logical or biblical argument against the movement?

7. If you're a critic of the seeker movement, does it make sense as based on the evidence that a stronger argument for your not favoring the movement is your personal preference? If not, why not? Shouldn't your view be that, while your preference is different, you wish Willow Creek and other biblically functioning seeker churches God's best? If not, why not?

8. If you're a critic, have you found yourself passing judgment on the movement contrary to what Paul says in Romans 14:13? If so, what will you do about this? If you plan to continue in your criticism, do you not fear the judgment of God?

9. Would you agree that giving up your worship service preference so that lost people can be reached is an example of servanthood? Are you willing to do this? If not, could this be a reason why you oppose the seeker movement or setting aside Sunday worship to reach lost people?

10. If you've been a critic of Willow Creek Community Church in particular based on many of the false arguments that the author has exploded, are you willing to repent before God for your

words and behavior? If you are a pastor and have spoken pub-
licly against Willow Creek Community Church, are you willing
to set the record straight?

11. Do you believe that the author's "critique of the critics" is fair?
Why or why not? What is his strongest point? What is his weak-
est point?

12. Do you consider yourself to be a critic of the new-model churches?
If yes, why? Has this chapter helped you at all? If so, in what
way? If not, what other help do you need?

13. If you are an admitted critic of new-model churches, do you believe that you can approach this topic fairly? Why or why not?
If not, what would it take for you to do so?

14. If you're a critic of any model of church, are you still open to
discussing the issues on an intellectual level? If not, why not?
What positive benefit does a close-minded approach have?

10

The Strategizing Church

Developing a New-Model Church

In the introduction to this book I asked, Is there a standard model for doing church? Does the Bible give us a correct, prescribed model that we're all to follow? By the time you've reached this chapter, you know that the biblical answer to this question is no. The Holy Spirit has given his church much freedom as to how it does church. Thus every church reflects a unique church model whether traditional or more contemporary. I believe that even those most critical of new-model churches would agree when they stop to think about it. Today's traditional models were yesterday's contemporary new-model churches, and they were criticized in their day. Today's new-model churches are tomorrow's traditional models, and it's likely that in time their adherents will be critical of future models.

Whether we like them or not, church models have always been with us and will continue to be with us until the Savior returns for us. Since God doesn't endorse a particular model of church, then an important question is, How should we develop new church models? What can we do to make sure they are based on and remain true to Scripture? In this chapter we'll look first at a common problem that faces new church models and discover how not to develop it. Then I'll provide the solution that is a process for developing future churches that will glorify the Savior.

The Problem Facing New Church Models

I've encountered a pattern that disturbs me. We discovered in chapter 1 that as many as 80 to 85 percent of America's churches are plateaued or in decline. If you look to the helm of these churches, you'll find a number of discouraged pastors who are attempting to lead their struggling churches. Hoping to find an answer to their dilemma or to discover a better way of doing church, often these leaders attend one of the many fine conferences put on by successful megachurch models, such as Saddleback Church, Willow Creek Community Church, North Point Church, and Oak Cliff Bible Fellowship.

The problem is that many of these pastors, desperate for an answer, become enamored with these highly successful models, return home, and attempt to implement them in their churches. Then they can't understand why several months later the church is seriously divided, split, or in some cases has run them off. They haven't taken into account that their church is not located in Southern California, Chicago, Atlanta, or Dallas, and that they aren't Rick Warren, Bill Hybels, Andy Stanley, or Tony Evans. My point is that a model that works well in one locale may not work at all somewhere else. And many of us do not have the leadership gifts and skills that other successful leaders have. Much the same happens with church planting when a gifted, godly church planter attempts to replicate one of these models somewhere in North America and beyond. My advice is to attend these conferences and learn from the models anything that may be helpful to your ministry situation, but don't mimic the model! We have no business franchising church models.

How to Develop New Church Models

So what is the solution? It's my view that the problem isn't with the model or its leadership. Though not without their own problems, these megachurches I've used as examples above are very fine, biblical ministries led by godly leadership teams. The answer to the dilemma of how to develop new church models is to develop biblically based models that are endemic or indigenous to one's own community and leadership. This is true for both church planting and the renewal of established churches.

The remaining question that begs to be answered is how might we develop such models? I've used the following process both as a pastor and as a consultant, and God in turn has used it to start new works (see my book *Planting Growing Churches for the 21st Century*[1]) and renew established works across North America and abroad (see *Advanced Strategic Planning*). I believe it is the process that Christ is using to build his church (see Matt. 16:18), and it leads us to develop new models. It consists of three phases (the three Ps): *preparation*, *process*, and *practice*.

The Preparation Phase

Before a church launches into the process of developing its model, it must do some preparation for the process. Lance Armstrong won the Tour de France several years in a row. We would all agree that this took much time and preparation that consisted of some grueling work. My point is that he didn't one day simply decide that he would enter the Tour de France and the next thing we know he's won it! The same holds true for churches as they develop their unique ministry models. I also highly recommend that the church work with a consultant who has had much experience with such processes. (I've included some information on consulting in appendix A for those who want to know more.) A consultant will save you much time and money and can address issues with your congregation that a pastor can't. If this isn't possible, then attend an offsite training venue, such as those that the Malphurs Group conducts to help leaders of smaller churches learn the process. You can find out more about these opportunities by going to my website (www.malphursgroup.com) or contacting me at Aubrey@malphursgroup.com.

This preparation phase consists of the following seven steps that will help leaders not only prepare their churches for change but assess whether the church is ready to move forward at this time in its life.

Step 1: Secure Support

Secure the support of the church's empowered leadership. I'm not using the term *empowered* in a negative way. Often when we hear the word *power*, we cringe. We must realize that power can be good or bad, depending on who has it and how he or she uses it. Here I'm referring to either use. Every church has people with power who use it knowingly or unknowingly for influence. They would include a governing board, the senior pastor, any staff persons, and a church patriarch or matriarch. It's important to the process of developing a new church model that most of these people be on board, especially the pastor and a strong governing board.

How do you find out if they're supportive? Ask them and see how they respond. Often their body language will tell you as much as their words. If they're hesitant or unsure, I've found that bringing in a knowledgeable consultant will help them understand the process better, answer their questions, and surface their need to move on with the process.

Step 2: Recruit a Team

The next step is to recruit a strategic leadership team (SLT). Many of us have discovered that leadership in the twenty-first century is much different than it was in much of the twentieth century, when people, especially the older, Builder generation, were willing to follow a single leader, such as a pastor. They trusted this person to lead them. With younger generations in the twenty-first century, much of this has changed. Now leadership is better accomplished through a team.

Recruit the primary spiritual and ministry leaders in your church to be on the strategic leadership team with the responsibility to lead the model development process. The size of this team will depend on the size of your church. Most teams range in size from ten to thirty people. When consulting, I prefer the larger team. Regardless of the number, the team members will be your church's gifted leaders, consisting of the pastor, any staff, a majority of the board, and the church's lay leaders, such as Sunday school teachers, small group leaders, and so on. Make sure that women are included on this team. They provide a critical leadership dimension to the church and are often underrepresented at the leadership level.

This team will be making lots of critical decisions. I advise you to take a consensus decision-making approach. Let people discuss and even debate the issues. Give people with differing viewpoints two or three minutes to present their positions. Then quickly move to make a decision. Let the team vote, and the majority wins the day.

Step 3: Communicate with the Congregation

Sometimes when we pursue a model development process, we forget to keep the congregation informed of what we're doing. As one leader says, "People who aren't up on something will be down on it!" The Malphurs Group has a saying: "You can't lead them if they don't trust you!" It's vital to the process that the congregation trust the process and the strategic leadership team. Initially you will generate lots of congregational trust because the people who influence them are on the team. However, you need to maintain that trust. To do this, seek to communicate formally and informally. A formal approach involves bulletin inserts, information in a newsletter, announcements from the pulpit, and so on. I also encourage pastors to interview the influential people on the SLT during the morning worship service. An informal approach is to encourage the SLT to tell others what they're doing after each meeting. You'll find that they will be excited about the process and delight in sharing it with those with whom they have influence.

Step 4: Assess Readiness

Assess the church's readiness for change. When a congregation goes through a remodeling process, most are aware that this means things will be changing. Your people will be somewhere along a continuum, ranging from a readiness to change right now to an unwillingness to accept any change at all (you may recall that I addressed this back in the introduction to this book). It's important that you determine how ready the church is to change, because this will serve to guide the modeling process. One way to do this is to have the team take a Readiness for Change Inventory, which I have provided for you in appendix B. You could give this to the entire church if it is a smaller church, say two hundred or fewer people. However, the team of leaders will likely be able to respond for the congregation, regardless of the size of the church.

It is imperative you provide your church with a biblical theology of change that will help them understand that it's okay to change and what should and shouldn't change. While this may help them intellectually to embrace change, it may or may not have an effect on those who oppose any change whatsoever at an emotional level.

You can use the theology of change that I presented in chapter 5. It consists of the three Fs: *function, form,* and *freedom.* As you'll recall, the functions of the church refer to such principles as evangelism, worship, and so on. These must never change. They must characterize the church regardless of the century it lives in. The forms are the various methods that churches use to implement the functions and are what make different models unique. The way one church worships may not be appropriate for another church in another part of the country. There is much room biblically for flexibility with the forms, and much is based on congregational preference.

Step 5: Conduct a Church Ministry Analysis

A church ministry analysis will help your team determine how the church is doing. A good one consists of both an internal and an external analysis. The internal analysis assesses how the church itself is doing. The external analysis looks at the church's community and tells the church what it needs to know about that community to reach it for Christ. The church must be aware of the community it is commissioned to reach. Both analyses are necessary to good church planting and renewal.

A good internal analysis will address the following areas:

- where the church is on the organizational life cycle (most are facing some kind of growth challenge—whether growing, plateaued, or declining)
- a performance audit that assesses the church's strengths and weaknesses
- a direction audit to determine if the church has a mission and vision
- a strategy audit to determine who the church wants to reach and how it plans to accomplish this
- an outreach audit to determine if the church is outward or inward focused
- a culture audit that helps the team understand the church's unique culture
- an obstacles audit to discover if there are any barriers in place that are derailing effective ministry
- an age audit to assess whether the church is balanced in terms of the age of its people
- an energy audit to measure the intensity with which people pursue ministry

- an emotions audit that determines whether the church is upbeat or downbeat emotionally
- a financial audit that assesses the church's financial circumstances

A good external analysis will touch on the following areas:

- a community audit that assesses how well the congregation understands its community
- an external threats audit that alerts the church to anything in the community that might threaten it in some way
- a competitor's audit that surfaces various events and organizations that will compete with the church for the hearts of its people
- an opportunities audit that discovers various opportunities in the community for ministry to that community

As a feature of my consulting ministry, I offer a ministry analysis that you can download and put online for your church to use. You can find it on my website (www.malphursgroup.com).

Step 6: Set Time Expectations

Set reasonable time expectations for developing the modeling process. Planting new-model churches and renewing old-model churches will not happen overnight. It's a gradual process that takes place over time. Older model churches didn't get that way overnight. The same holds true for those desiring to transition to and implement a newer model. Some changes will take place immediately. Others will take some time. My research and experience say that it will take at least three years and sometimes as long as eight years for a church to embrace a new model. This calls for pastors who will stay for the long haul and for congregations who will be patient with the process.

Step 7: Lay a Spiritual Foundation

A vital aspect of planting a new-model church or renewing an older model ministry is spiritual formation, which must and will undergird the process. Use this process as an opportunity to call the church in general and the SLT in particular to spiritual revival and renewal. When I work with an SLT, I help them individually work through the following areas:

- acknowledge their personal sinfulness (Ps. 51:5; Rom. 7:14; 1 John 1:8, 10)
- confess their sins to God (Psalm 51; 1 John 1:9)
- forgive those who may have wronged them (Matt. 18:21–22; Eph. 4:31–32)
- pray for themselves and the church (Matt. 7:7–12; James 5:16)
- put off any negative "stuff," especially complaining (1 Cor. 10:10; Eph. 4:1–3, 29; Phil. 2:14)
- agree to church discipline (Matt. 18:15–20; 1 Cor. 5:1–13)
- obey their church leadership, including the pastor (1 Thess. 5:12–13; Heb. 13:17)
- strive for church unity (Eph. 4:1–16; John 17:11)
- listen to others (James 1:19–21)
- speak the truth in love (Eph. 4:15)
- pursue holiness (Rom. 6:1–14; 12:1–2)
- be servants (Matt. 20:20–28; Phil. 2:3–11)
- remember that the church belongs to Christ and not to us (Matt. 16:18)

The Process Phase

Once the team has worked through the preparation phase, it should be ready to launch the actual model developing process. The process that I've developed and use consists of four steps: core values discovery, mission development, vision development, and the articulation of a strategy to implement the mission and vision.

Step 1: Discover Your Core Values

Discovering your church's core values will help the church understand why it does what it does or doesn't do what it should do. Core values explain who you are—your core ministry identity. As your cells' DNA provides the building blocks of your physical body, so your church's DNA provides the building blocks of the church. I've always told churches that if they can tell me their core values, I can tell them everything about their church.

The definition of core values. I define core values as *the constant, passionate, biblical core beliefs that drive the church.* They're constant because they are very slow to change. This is one reason the change process can take so long—it often involves changing and embracing new values at the church's core. Core values are passionate because they touch people deeply at an emotional level. We feel strongly and care deeply about these values. And core values are biblical. They are the church's core beliefs and are central to the ministry, so most of the values of a church should be found in the Bible and agree with the Bible. Finally, values drive the ministry. They move the ministry in some direction. That direction is the church's mission. Should a church be off course and not pursuing a Great Commission mission, then the problem lies with the values. They aren't in line with the church's professed mission.

Usually a church has only four to six core values. Some churches list as many as twelve to sixteen, but usually when this many are listed, some aren't core values.

The kinds of core values. There are several different kinds of values that exist in tension.

- Conscious versus unconscious values. The church's core beliefs most often lie at an unconscious level—people aren't aware of them. Thus it becomes the leaders' or consultant's responsibility to help them discover and articulate those values, raising them from an unconscious to a conscious level.
- Shared versus unshared values. A ministry's shared values are those on which most of the people agree. They are essential to ministry effectiveness, while unshared values bring ministry demise.
- Personal versus organizational values. People have their own personal values, and ministry organizations have values. Since churches are organizations that consist of people, the church's values consist of the sum of its people's shared values. Therefore, you would be wise to make sure that all staff and any new members to the church agree with or are in alignment with the church's essential shared values.
- Actual versus aspirational values. Actual values are the beliefs people own and practice daily. An example would be the Jerusalem church's values as articulated in Acts 2:42–47. Aspirational values are beliefs that the congregation doesn't own or practice. For example, a church may believe that evangelism is an actual core value, but they've won no one to faith in years. In many cases they know it should be an actual value, so they identify it

as such. However, the fact that they do not regularly share their faith and see people come to the Lord reveals that evangelism is not an actual value.

- Single versus multiple values. While most ministries have several or multiple values, some have one that towers above all the rest and dominates them. This demonstrates the power of a value. An example would be biblical doctrine. This is the central, dominating value in the teaching church. The pastor teaches biblical doctrine, and everyone expects him to do it well. Should he focus on another value, he is out of sync with the congregation.

The discovery of core values. Once you know why values are important to your congregation and what they are, it's imperative that you identify your church's core values. You need to know what is driving your church and ultimately where it's going. This is the responsibility of the strategic leadership team. In my book *Advanced Strategic Planning*, I elaborate on several different approaches to discovering a church's core values. However, the simplest way is to take a core values audit, and I have provided one for you in appendix C.

Step 2: Develop Your Mission

Once a church knows its core values, the next step is to develop a mission. A mission is important because it dictates the ministry's direction. Therefore one of the first jobs of a leader is to help the ministry think through and define its mission. It must answer the questions, What are we supposed to be doing? What is our mission in and to our ministry community?

The definition of a mission. I define a church's mission as *a broad, brief, biblical statement of what the ministry is supposed to be doing.* It's made up of four key elements:

- A mission is broad. A good mission is expansive, comprehensive, and overarching. It's the goal of all goals and includes under it all that the church does as a ministry. It forms the umbrella that covers all its other ministry activities.
- A mission is brief. No doubt you've seen a number of mission statements that are rather lengthy. And some people even encourage this. However, I believe that we are wise to take Peter Drucker's advice: a mission must be short enough to fit on a T-shirt. A

primary reason is that you want your people to remember the church's mission, and they won't even bother to remember a long mission statement. Would you?

- A mission is biblical. God determines the church's mission. And the Savior dictated that mission more than two thousand years ago when he said, "Make disciples!" (see Matt. 28:19–20).
- Finally, a mission addresses what your ministry is supposed to be doing. That way your people know what they are supposed to be doing, what's expected of them. It's Christ's Great Commission.

The development of a mission. It's the job of the leadership in general and the SLT in particular to develop the church's mission statement. Following are four guidelines that will help facilitate this:

- Determine what your church is supposed to be doing. As I've said above as well as in other chapters, the church that follows the Bible has little option. What it is supposed to be doing is making disciples. Whatever words the ministry chooses to use to express the statement, the Great Commission must be at the core of it.
- Articulate the mission in writing. Some leaders will tell you that their churches have a mission, but if they can't write it down, they don't have one, at least not a clear one. Your mission will not have the authority of a leadership statement until it's clear enough to be committed to paper.
- Clarify your mission. As you develop your mission, use language that's not only biblically accurate but language that your people can understand. Also, either avoid or define biblical terms, such as *disciple*, *glorify*, and *holy*. While these are perfectly good biblical terms, they're abstract and most people don't really understand what they mean. For example, if you asked ten people to say what a disciple is, you would likely get ten different answers. If you decide to use such terms, then clarify what you mean by them. Observe how Willow Creek Community Church has done this with their mission statement: "To turn irreligious people into *fully devoted followers of Christ*." In this statement the concept of a disciple is fully explained.
- Keep your mission statement short and simple. My friend and fellow consultant Will Mancini put it this way: "Say more by saying less." Again, you want people to remember your mission statement. Here's a mission statement that is short and memorable:

"Our mission is to know Christ and make him known." Another church developed the following statement: "To passionately follow and make followers of Christ." If you desire to see more examples of mission statements, my book *Advanced Strategic Planning* contains a number of them in its section on mission.

Step 3: Develop Your Vision

The third step in the model developing process is to develop a church vision. While you aren't able to predict your church's future, you can create it within the sovereignty of God. And the way you accomplish this is to develop a vision.

The definition of a vision. I define a vision as *a clear, challenging picture of the future of a church, as you believe that it can and must be.* It contains five essentials:

- A vision is clear. We can't expect people to act on what they don't understand. Vision clarity is essential to vision accomplishment, and a vision accomplishes nothing if it isn't clear and concise.
- A vision is challenging. A good vision connects with your people. It ignites their passion and compels them to action. It pulls them out of the pews and into the arena of effective ministry.
- A vision is a picture of the future of your ministry. While passion is a feeling word, vision is a seeing word. It helps people visualize where the ministry is going, making them want to be a part of that future. It's what you see when you think of the church five, ten, or twenty years in the future.
- A vision can be. A good vision drips with potential. It involves not what is but what could be. Robert Kennedy once said, "Some people see things the way they are and ask why; I see things the way they could be and ask why not." This sentiment characterizes visionary leaders and their churches.
- Finally a vision must be. A good vision won't let go. It grabs hold of our hearts and compels us to act until it becomes a reality.

The development of a vision. There are at least three ways you and your team can develop a vision statement for your ministry.

- Expand your mission statement. With this approach, you return to the mission statement you developed in step 2 and use it as a foundation on which to build your vision statement. Here are key questions: What will our church be like when we begin to realize our mission? What do we see? What could be?

- Build on your core values. With this approach, you return to your core values that you discovered in step 1. Then you ask, What will our church look like when it begins to accomplish each core value in the lives of its people?

- Model your vision after another vision. You may be aware of another church's vision that excites you and would make an excellent vision for your church as well. I suggest that you not embrace the entire vision because every church is different. Instead, take the vision statement and tweak it until you can identify with it and it becomes your own.

Step 4: Develop Your Strategy

Once you have a mission and vision, you need to develop a strategy to accomplish them. Both the mission and vision answer the question, What are we supposed to be doing? The strategy answers the question, How will we accomplish what we're supposed to be doing? I break the strategy step into the following elements.

Discover your ministry community. To discover your ministry community you must answer the question, Whom will we reach? This is essentially an Acts 1:8 exercise: What is your Jerusalem, Judea, Samaria, and the ends of the earth? The answer to this question is fourfold:

- You need to identify who lives in your community. You can accomplish this through a community analysis that examines your community's demographics and psychographics. Determine the boundaries of your community. For most it will be their city or county, depending on their size.

- How many people will you reach in your community? Once you have a feel for the number of unchurched people in your community, ask two questions. How many people in our community can we expose to the gospel? And how many can we win to faith in Christ? The latter figure is often around 10 percent of those living in the community, which is doable for most churches.

- You should determine what kind of church it will take to reach your community. Ask what kind of pastor it will take, what kind of people, programs, and so forth.

- You need to know how to position yourself to reach your community. This addresses how people will discover your presence in the community and your image in light of that presence. You'll need to communicate with them through a logo, tagline, signs, mailers, word of mouth, and so on.

Make mature disciples. Once you know whom you're trying to reach, you need to come up with a process that enables them to become Christ's disciples. This process takes several steps. First, return to your mission statement and ask, What are the characteristics of a mature disciple? What does one look like? Limit them to four and articulate them through alliteration or an acrostic. The last church I pastored used alliteration and came up with four characteristics represented by four Cs: *conversion, community, commitment,* and *contribution.*

Second, create what I refer to as a maturity matrix. It consists of a horizontal line along which you place the characteristics of a mature disciple (your ends), and a vertical line on which you list the primary ministry activities that you believe will accomplish those characteristics in the lives of your congregation and community (your means to accomplish your ends). These will be such main featured activities as your worship time, Sunday school, small groups, and so on. Here's the critical question: Are your ministry means (activities) accomplishing in some way your ministry ends (your characteristics of a disciple)? If not, you need to evaluate and if necessary change some of your means. Here's an example of a maturity matrix:

		Conversion	Community	Commitment	Contribution
A					
C	Worship service	√		√	
T					
I	Sunday school			√	
V					
I	Small groups		√		
T					
I	Mobilization ministry				√
E					
S					

Third, measure the church's spiritual progress. The way to determine if God is using and blessing your process is to measure it. Remember, what gets measured is what gets done! You could do this the way they did in the New Testament. For example, the churches in Acts measured their efforts at evangelism by tracking the number of baptisms (Acts 2:41; 8:12–16, for example).

Develop a ministry dream team. Once you know whom you want to reach (your ministry community) and what you want to do for them (make them disciples), you need to develop a dream team with a vision to accomplish this. A dream team may consist of as many as three groups: a governing board, a staff, and the lay volunteers and leaders who do the actual ministry.

Some churches have a governing board and some don't. The advantage of such a board is wisdom and pastoral accountability. A wise pastor will cultivate such a board and make sure that it supports his or her ministry strategy and general direction of the church. All churches will have a staff. The staff may include only a part-time, bivocational pastor and a secretary or hundreds of people staffing a megachurch. It's imperative that a church have staff who align with the values, mission, vision, and general strategy of the church, including style of worship. Too many senior pastors make the mistake of hiring the wrong staff or not developing the existing staff.

Vital to the success of any church is the involvement of its lay leaders and people in its ministry. Pastors need to make congregational mobilization a priority of their ministry to these people. That is one of their responsibilities according to Ephesians 4:11–13.

Determine the best ministry setting. A ministry setting consists of the church's location and facilities. Now that you know the people in the community that you may best reach, evaluate the location of your facilities in light of where these people are located in your community. Are you located in the best place to reach them? Your facilities are also critical to reaching your community for the Savior. Have you taken good care of your facilities, and are they adequate for your ministries? An issue to consider if you are growing is whether you've maximized your facilities or when this might happen. The key is doing something about this before it happens; otherwise, when your facilities are filled to capacity, you will experience a plateau and likely a decline in your growth.

Raise the necessary finances. It will take money to reach your community with your team through your disciple-making process. In our North American culture, it is usually the job of the church's senior pastor to raise the ministry funds. Most pastors don't like to hear this, because they have no formal training in fund-raising and simply don't like to do it.

To successfully raise funds, a pastor needs to know how much to raise. The answer is found in the budget, but not just any budget will do. It needs to be aligned with the ministry's core values and mission. Then the pastor needs to know how to raise these funds. Here is a general overview of how to do this:

- Articulate a biblical theology of finances.
- Regularly cast the church's vision.
- Implement a churchwide stewardship ministry.
- Regularly communicate with the congregation about the financial condition of the church.
- Conduct capital funds campaigns.
- Cultivate champions (those with the gift of giving).

There isn't enough space in this chapter to go into detail on each of these fund-raising points or on the other elements above that make up the strategy. I address each in much more detail in chapter 12 of *Advanced Strategic Planning,* and Pastor Steve Stroope and I address the complete picture of finances in our book *Money Matters.*[2]

The Practice Phase

Now that the team has worked through the preparation for and process of church model building, they come to the practice phase. It consists of two steps—implementing and then evaluating the new model.

Step 1: Implement the New-Model Church

You could develop the finest, most biblical model ever for a church, but without implementation, your plan would just sit in some dusty church filing cabinet in the church office. Nothing would ever happen. There are eight parts to implementation:

- Formulate your implementation goals. At this point, collect all the goals that have surfaced in the above strategizing process.
- Determine specific priorities. Determine which are essential to effectively implement the ministry strategy, and prioritize them.

- Communicate the goals to the congregation. They need to be aware of what you are doing and the reasons so that they can support and pray for the implementation of the model.
- Articulate specific, measurable actions. Determine the actions that you plan to take to accomplish each goal.
- Decide on a deadline. When must each action item be accomplished?
- Assign responsible persons who will see that each action is accomplished.
- Provide the necessary resources. These resources include time, finances, facilities, and tools. Do the responsible persons have the necessary resources?
- Establish MIR meetings. MIR stands for monthly implementation review, which describes what the meetings are about. This is a time when people report on their progress or the lack thereof. It also brings accountability to the implementation process as well as encouragement and praise.

Step 2: Evaluate the New-Model Church

Very few churches conduct formal evaluations, but whether they want it or not, all are evaluated informally. Visitors as well as the current congregation evaluate them every Sunday after the service. Inwardly and often vocally they ask, *Did I like what just took place? Was God present?* Since people are informally evaluating our services, I believe that we would be wise to formally evaluate our services.

There are several reasons for evaluation:

- It lets us know how we're doing. Are our ministries accomplishing what we want them to? Where do we need to tweak them?
- It lets us know how our people are doing. Are they becoming mature disciples?
- Evaluation encourages affirmation. It provides us with an opportunity to say thanks for a job well done.
- It promotes change. If we regularly tweak our ministries to make them better, then we're constantly changing what we're doing so that we continually become a better church that is serving Christ more effectively.

You will want to evaluate the ministers—all the people who are involved in some way with the church's ministry. Staff, laypersons, and visitors should all be involved in the evaluation. Ask, How are our ministers doing? What are they doing well? Do we need to give them a raise as well as some praise? Where are they struggling, and what can we do to help them? Are they involved in the right ministry for them, or should they consider a move to another ministry? Ask visitors for a brief response to what they experienced in their time with you.

The ministries are the church's activities that make up its strategy to accomplish its mission-vision. Ask, How are our ministries doing? Are they helping our people to become mature disciples? Every ministry has a shelf life; have any of our ministries reached that point? What new ministries do we need?

In a number of places in this chapter I have referred you to my book *Advanced Strategic Planning*, because it covers in 367 pages what I've attempted to cover as an overview in this one chapter. If you would like more information on a particular area, you will find it in that book.

Questions for Reflection and Discussion

1. Are you more comfortable in an older or a new-model church? Why do you prefer the one you do? How does your preference affect your feelings toward other models? Do you find yourself at times being critical? Is this fair? Why or why not? If you think you are being unfair, what will you do about it?

2. Do you agree that we must develop new-model churches? If yes, why? If not, why not?

3. Have you been involved in developing a new-model church? If so, was your experience a good one or a bad one? Why? If you had an opportunity to do it again, would you? Why or why not?

4. Do you believe that the author's concern about pastors and leaders adopting models that aren't representative of or indigenous to their communities is valid? Why or why not?

5. What do you like about the author's *preparation phase*? Do you agree that it is important to have a team through which to lead? How important is communication to the process? Why? What do you dislike about it?

6. What do you like about the author's *process phase*? Do you feel he has touched the primary bases that need to be touched (values, mission, vision, and strategy)? What don't you like about it?

7. What do you like about the *practice phase*? Do you agree that without it, much of the planning will never be implemented? Do you believe that evaluation is important? Why? What do you not like about this phase?

8. Do you believe that this process will work in your situation? Why or why not?

Appendix A

Church Consulting

Why Using a Church Consultant
Is a Good Investment for Your Ministry

Have you ever struggled with the idea of bringing in someone as a ministry consultant when you know that you are in over your head? Ever found it difficult to convince a board or a church treasurer that you need some specialized help? While in seminary, I worked for a Christian businessman who regularly brought in a business consultant to help him with the operation of his company. As I look back on that, I realize the wisdom of such coaching and consulting. So did various leaders in the Scriptures—Moses had Jethro (Exodus 18) and Timothy and Titus had Paul. The following are several value-added features that argue strongly for using a ministry consultant.

A good church consultant has the experience, expertise, and time that your leadership staff simply don't have. The advent of ministry learning organizations, the explosion of knowledge, and the fast pace of communication make it nearly impossible for a senior pastor or an executive leadership team to remain knowledgeable of new methods and ministry paradigms that God is blessing. In addition, projects that require new skills and lots of time bombard leaders almost daily. In today's fast-paced, ever-changing world, churches have difficulty hiring enough knowledgeable people just to keep up with normal, ongoing ministries. Strategic-minded churches and other ministry organizations are increasingly turning to ministry consultants to help them fill the knowledge and time gap for the many special situations that arise. These consultants bring their expertise and years of ministry experience gained from other projects and other ministry organizations.

A good church consultant provides flexibility for their client churches. The typical church can bring in a consultant for short-term knowledge acquisition, skills development, strategic planning, and other ministry projects. Much as Jethro in Exodus 18:14–27, they're there when you need them and gone when you don't. They come on the scene, serve your purpose, and then disappear. That way they do not get underfoot. Many also offer coaching over the telephone or Internet that is flexible to a leader's time.

A good church consultant provides a fresh, objective point of view. Most consultants have other projects under their belt and valuable experience in dealing with an array of ministry situations and leadership personalities. These provide them with fresh, unbiased approaches to ministry. This "cross-pollination" of ideas and experiences from other similar ministries allows you to tap into the brainpower and strategies of those ministries. Often the pastor or leadership staff are too close to their situation to see the problems and potential solutions that a good, objective consultant recognizes almost immediately. In addition, the consultant doesn't have to tolerate but can address any internal politics or power plays that some use to short-circuit healthy, biblical change.

A good church consultant provides maximum ministry efficiency. There are three reasons they can do this. First, they bring experience with similar situations or problems so that they don't need to take valuable time to get up to speed. Second, senior pastors, other leadership staff, or volunteer leaders have to accomplish their "normal" assignments in addition to any special projects. To become knowledgeable and give attention to a special project on top of many other responsibilities will usually be too much for a staff person to do well. Consultants, however, have the luxury of focusing all their expertise only on the special projects and assignments for which you've retained them. Third, they don't have to deal with the church's necessary, daily tasks, such as attending staff meetings, returning phone calls or answering emails from congregants, putting out fires, and dealing with policies and procedures. Armed with ministry tools, such as the storyboarding process, they complete their assignments in one-half to one-fourth the time it would take a staff person.

Finally, a good church consultant brings a solid grounding in the Bible and theology to the ministry situation. Ministry with and to churches is deeply theological. It's critical that a consultant have a thorough grounding in theology that he or she brings to your situation. We have discovered that good biblical, theological preparation is vital to the consulting equation. That is why the Malphurs Group uses only consultants who have been trained theologically in a seminary context.

Why Use a Consultant for Strategic Planning?

Some object to using a consultant to help them accomplish strategic planning because of the cost. They ask one of two questions. First, can we afford it? You would be wise to review how your church is doing. Is it growing, plateaued, or declining? If it's stuck or struggling in some way, then perhaps the question becomes, Can we afford not to work with such a person?

The second question is who's the cheapest? Those who are brand-new to church consulting and those who are just beginning to learn the field may be the cheapest, but let's face it, the old maxim "You get what you pay for" also applies to the church world in general and ministry consulting in particular.

Some churches recruit a person from within. However, if the project doesn't go well or even fails, you need to be aware that you won't get a second chance. If you bring it up again in the future, people will be quick to remind you, "We already tried that once and it didn't work!" It's wise to bring the best, most experienced resources to the process, because there likely won't be a second chance should it go poorly.

If the person who leads this planning project is a staff person, does he or she have the time over and above the normal load that the project will require? Is it fair to ask a staff person to take on this responsibility in addition to the normal staff duties that already fill his or her day? In addition, does the person have the expertise in strategic planning and theology that are needed to do a credible, Christ-honoring job?

If the person who leads you is a church member (possibly with some background in corporate strategic planning), does the person have the time that is required over and above his or her regular job? More important, does he or she have a good knowledge of the Bible and theology (strategic planning is deeply theological) as well as expertise in the specialized field of strategic church planning? (Strategic planning in the corporate world is very different from that in the church world.) If not, where and when will this person get this biblical knowledge and necessary expertise?

Most would agree that using a theologically trained, proven specialist in strategic church planning is the best way to go. Therefore, are you willing to settle for second or third best? Should the church of Jesus Christ ever settle for second best? The church is the only hope of a lost and dying world. Therefore, isn't your church worthy of your best efforts?

Qualifications of a Church Consultant

It's critical to the accomplishment of your ministry goals that you do your homework before selecting a church consultant and know what qualifications he or she should have. What are some of the qualities that distinguish the good ones from others in the field? Here are a few things that you'd be wise to check out.

Christian character. Does the consultant know Jesus Christ as personal Savior? Though non-Christian consultants can provide some excellent help in their chosen areas of expertise, Christian consultants should bring spiritual discernment to the consulting arena as well as expertise. Just as important is a second question: Is he or she living a life marked by Christlikeness? Consultants model behavior for those with whom they minister, and it's critical that it be Christlike behavior.

Proven competence. What are the consultant's primary areas of expertise? Some consultants minister in several different areas. However, most are experts and are known for their work in just a few specific areas. Look for one that is most competent in the area where you need him or her. Often, they'll be known for those areas, and some have published in them. Sometimes you may have to inquire. A consultant's references will clue you in to his or her areas of proven competence.

Theological expertise. You would be wise to examine the consultant's theological credentials. Does the consultant have any academic training in the Bible and theology? Few do, and the popular approach today is to put down academics. However, a person's academic preparation in theology serves to mold his or her thinking and ministry. Our group has discovered that good biblical, theological preparation is vital to the consulting equation. That is because strategic ministry planning is deeply theological. So you should find out if the consultant has gone to a Bible college and/or seminary. If so, where? Is it a reputable school? Evangelical? What degrees does the consultant have? Does he or she have a solid foundation in Bible and theology to bring to the consulting experience?

Strong references. A consultant should have references who can attest to the quality of his or her services. It's imperative that you talk with those who have worked with the consultant. To a certain extent, consultants function much as another staff person, and you must check their references much as you would those of a new staff person. Beware of those who have no references or have questionable references.

Special gifting. What are the gifts, talents, and abilities that the consultant brings to your ministry context? Some excellent gifts for consulting are leadership, administration, wisdom, and discernment mixed with lots of good, practical experience. While you're at it, check on the consultant's passions. (Passion is what you feel strongly about, what you care deeply about.) What is he or she passionate about? This passion will excite your people and rub off on them. When your people work with a consultant, will they come away excited or discouraged about what's ahead?

Practical experience. Discern how much experience the consultant has had. Is the person just beginning to use his or her gifts and abilities in the consulting world? Has the consultant ever pastored a church or worked with a parachurch organization? If so, when and for how long? While it's critical that a consultant start somewhere, maybe that first or second organization shouldn't be yours. How can you know? Ask for and check out their references. In addition, here are two disclaimers that you should jot down on your mental list. First, just because a consultant has a lot of experience doesn't mean that it is good experience. People can learn from bad experiences, but they learn more from good experiences. Second, contrary to popular opinion, star performers don't necessarily make the best consultants. There's often a big gap between being a great leader and coaching others to do the same. That's the reason so few star athletes become coaches.

Name recognition. What might seem like an unusual qualification is name recognition. When you think about the area in which you need a consultant's expertise, whose name usually rises to the surface? Who is known to be a leader in the field? When you ask knowledgeable people, whom do they suggest? There's a reason for this that is summed up in two words: proven expertise. While it doesn't have to be, most often the best consultant will be someone who has demonstrated competence by ministering and writing in the field under a credible, recognized publisher. The consultant writes out of a passion for the work and wants to share his or her competence with others.

Seven Reasons You Can Afford a Good Church Consultant

Why bring in a ministry consultant when a good one costs so much? Would you find it difficult to convince a board or a church treasurer that you need and can afford some specialized help? There are several reasons you can afford to bring in a competent, skilled church consultant.

1. *Rather than ask if you can afford a qualified consultant, the better question is, Can you afford* not *to work with a consultant?* Has the ministry reached a point where it is seriously at risk? Are you at a place where you need the expertise of a specialist? No one can know it all. Are you stuck in a problem or facing a daunting growth challenge, and the future of the ministry is hanging in the balance? It is likely that the future of the ministry rests with a wise decision to bring in outside help, such as a Jethro or a Paul.

2. *The benefit of a good consultant should more than pay for the cost of the service.* An aspect of the consultant's work should address the church's finances. The expertise of the consultant here should increase the church's income enough to more than cover his remuneration and expenses. We at the Malphurs Group address financial issues, such as the implementation of biblical stewardship programs and additional, alternative sources of funding. The long-term effect of such programs, along with renewed spiritual vigor, is to increase giving and thus the church's income substantially.

3. *Often there are those in the church who are willing to underwrite the cost of a consultant.* Initially most look to the church to cover the costs of a consultant. Have you thought about approaching someone or several people with the gift of giving and asking for their help? Still another option would be to ask them to match what the church pays for consulting. James says that you have

not because you ask not (4:2). Who in your congregation might be willing to cover these expenses if you asked them?

4. *Remember that you get what you pay for.* Perhaps you have discovered this truth in the business world. The same holds true in the world of church consulting. Each consultant varies in terms of qualifications. Some are gifted and have vast experience while others should not be in the consulting ministry. Most often you can tell the difference by their costs. Usually a good consultant will cost more, much more, than a mediocre one. And you have to ask if you are willing to entrust your church to mediocre. That is important to keep in mind when you shop church consultants.

5. *If you are a small church and find that you don't have the finances to bring in a consultant, consider combining with another church or two in your community and share the experience.* You and other churches could meet and plan together with the consultant and share the expense. Thus what may have seemed unaffordable becomes affordable and available through shared expenses, and you have multiple kingdom impact in your community. Another option is the Malphurs Group offsite training that costs less. (See our website for more information.)

6. *The need for consulting, and not the cost, should be the major issue.* Often churches that inquire about consulting ask first about the cost. This is a question that must be asked, but it shouldn't be the first question. For example, if you were struggling physically, you would make an appointment with your doctor. Suppose that he told you that you had cancer, and he recommended three doctors (oncologists). Would your first question be, Who is the cheapest? The same principle applies to our churches when they are struggling spiritually. The need is so great that the cost pales in significance.

7. *Finally, when it comes to the bottom line, a good church consultant is more cost effective for the ministry organization.* When the question is which is more cost efficient—using a consultant or hiring a new staff person—the answer is the consultant. Hired staff require a regular paycheck along with other benefits, such as a health package, retirement, and possibly a severance package. However, consultants serve you much as another staff person without the additional overhead. They work with you on an as-needed basis. The ministry has the benefit of an additional, specialized staff person without all the added financial overhead that comes with new staff.

Appendix B

Readiness for Change Inventory

Directions: Each item below is a key element that will help you evaluate your church's readiness for change. Strive for objectivity—involve others (including outsiders) in the evaluation process. Circle the number that most accurately rates your church.

1. **Leadership.** The pastor and the church board (official leadership) are favorable toward and directly responsible for change. Also, any influential persons (unofficial leadership: the church patriarch, a respected member, etc.) are for change—score 5. If moderately so—score 3. Only the secondary level of leadership (staff other than the pastor and board, Sunday school teachers, etc.) is for change, while unofficial leadership opposes it—score 1.

   5   3   1

2. **Vision.** The pastor and the board have a single, clear vision of a significant future that looks different from the present. The pastor is able to mobilize others (staff, boards, and the congregation) for action—score 5. The pastor but not the board envisions a different direction for the church—score 3. The pastor and board have not thought about a vision, and/or they do not believe that it is important—score 1.

   5   3   1

3. **Values.** The church's philosophy of ministry (its core values) includes a preference for innovation and creativity. Though proven forms, methods, and techniques are not quickly discarded, the church is more concerned with the effectiveness of

its ministries than with adherence to traditions—score 5. If moderately so—score 3. The church's ministry forms and techniques have changed little over the years, while its ministry effectiveness has diminished—score 1.

5   3   1

4. **Motivation.** The pastor and the board have a strong sense of urgency for change that is shared by the congregation. The congregational culture emphasizes the need for constant improvement—score 3. The pastor and/or the board (most of whom have been in their positions for many years) along with the congregation are bound by long-standing traditions that are change resistant and discourage risk taking—score 1. If somewhere between—score 2.

3   2   1

5. **Organizational Context.** How does the change effort affect the other programs in the church (Christian education, worship, missions, etc.)? If the individuals in charge are all working together for improvement and innovation—score 3. If only some are—score 2. If many are opposed to change and/or are in conflict with one another over change—score 1.

3   2   1

6. **Processes/Functions.** Major changes in a church almost always require redesigning processes and functions in all the ministries of the church, such as Christian education and church worship. If most in charge of these areas are open to change—

score 3. If only some—score 2. If they are turf protectors or if they put their areas of ministry ahead of the church as a whole—score 1.

3   2   1

7. **Ministry Awareness.** Does the leadership of your church keep up with what is taking place in the innovative evangelical churches in the community and across America in terms of ministry and outreach effectiveness? Does the leadership objectively compare the church's ministry with that of churches very similar to it? If the answer is yes— score 3. If the answer is sometimes—score 2. If no—score 1.

3   2   1

8. **Community Focus.** Does the church know and understand the people in the community—their needs, hopes, aspirations? Does it stay in direct contact with them? Does it regularly seek to reach them? If the answer is yes—score 3. If moderately so—score 2. If the church is not in touch with its community and focuses primarily on itself—score 1.

3   2   1

9. **Evaluation.** Does the church regularly evaluate its ministries? Does it evaluate its ministries in light of its vision and goals? Are these ministries regularly adjusted in response to the evaluations? If all of this takes place—score 3. If some takes place—score 2. If none— score 1.

3   2   1

10. **Rewards.** Change is easier if the leaders and those involved in

ministry are rewarded in some way for taking risks and looking for new solutions to their ministry problems. Rewarding ministry teams is more effective than rewarding solo performances. If your church gives rewards—score 3. If sometimes—score 2. If your church rewards the status quo and has only a maintenance mentality—score 1.

3   2   1

11. **Organizational Structure.** The best situation is a flexible church where change is well received and takes place periodically, not every day. If this is true of your church—score 3. If your church is very rigid in its structure and either has changed very little in the last five years or has experienced several futile attempts at change to no avail—score 1. If between—score 2.

3   2   1

12. **Communication.** Does your church have a variety of means for two-way communication? Do most people understand and use it, and does it reach all levels of the congregation? If all of this is true—score 3. If only moderately true—score 2. If communication is poor, primarily one-way and from the top down—score 1.

3   2   1

13. **Organizational Hierarchy.** Is your church decentralized (there are few if any levels of leadership between the congregation and the pastor or the board)? If so—score 3. If there are people on staff levels or boards/committees who come between the congregation and the pastor or the

board, then more potential exists for them to block essential change—score 1. If between—score 2.

3   2   1

14. **Prior Change.** Churches will most readily adapt to change if they have successfully implemented major changes in the recent past. If this is true of your church—score 3. If some change has taken place—score 2. If no one can remember the last time the church changed or if such efforts at change failed or left people angry and resentful—score 1.

3   2   1

15. **Morale.** Do the church staff and volunteers enjoy the church and take responsibility for their ministries? Do they trust the pastor and/or the board? If so—score 3. If moderately so—score 2. Do few people volunteer, and are there signs of low team spirit? Is there mistrust between leaders and followers and between the various ministries? If so—score 1.

3   2   1

16. **Innovation.** The church tries new things. People feel free to implement new ideas on a consistent basis. People have the freedom to make choices and solve problems regarding their ministries. If this describes your church—score 3. If this is somewhat true—score 2. If ministries are ensnared in bureaucratic red tape and if permission from "on high" must be obtained before anything happens—score 1.

3   2   1

17. **Decision Making.** Does the church leadership listen carefully to a wide variety of suggestions from all the congregation? After it has gathered the appropriate information, does it make decisions quickly? If so—score 3. If moderately so—score 2. Does the leadership listen only to a select few and take forever to make a decision? Is there lots of conflict during the process, and after a decision is made, is there confusion and turmoil?—score 1.

         3   2   1

Total score: _____

If your score is:

47–57: The chances are good that you (the senior pastor or key leader) may implement change, especially if your scores are high on items 1–3.

28–46: Change may take place but with varying success. Chances increase with higher scores on items 1–3. Note areas with low scores and focus on improvement before attempting change on a large scale.

17–27: Change will likely not take place. Note areas with low scores and attempt to improve them if possible. Consider starting a new church and implement your ideas in a more change-friendly context.

Appendix C

Church Ministry Core Values Audit

Directions: Using the scale below, circle the number that best expresses to what extent the following values are important to your church (actual values). Work your way through the list quickly, going with your first impression.

1 = not important		
2 = somewhat important		
3 = important		
4 = most important		

1. **Preaching and teaching Scripture:** Communicating God's Word to people.   1   2   3   4

2. **Family:** People immediately related to one another by marriage or birth.   1   2   3   4

3. **Bible knowledge:** A familiarity with the truths of the Scriptures.   1   2   3   4

4. **World missions:** Spreading the gospel of Christ around the globe.   1   2   3   4

5. **Community:** Caring about and addressing the needs of others.   1   2   3   4

6. **Encouragement:** Giving hope to people who need some hope.   1   2   3   4

7. **Giving:** Providing a portion of one's finances to support the ministry.   1   2   3   4

8. **Fellowship:** Relating to and enjoying one another.   1   2   3   4

9. **Leadership:** A person's ability to influence others to pursue God's mission for their organization.   1   2   3   4

10. **Cultural relevance:** Communicating truth in a way that people who aren't like us understand it.   1   2   3   4

11. **Prayer:** Communicating with God.   1   2   3   4

12. **Excellence:** Maintaining the highest of ministry standards that bring glory to God.   1   2   3   4

13. **Evangelism:** Telling others the good news about Christ.   1   2   3   4

14. **Team ministry:** A group of people ministering together.   1   2   3   4

15. **Creativity:** Coming up with new ideas and ways of doing ministry.   1   2   3   4

16. **Worship:** Attributing worth to God.   1   2   3   4

17. **Status quo:** A preference for the way things are now.   1   2   3   4

18. **Cooperation:** The act of working together in the service of the Savior.   1   2   3   4

19. **Lost people:** People who are non-Christians and may not attend church (unchurched).   1   2   3   4

20. **Mobilized laity:** Christians who are actively serving in the ministries of their church.   1   2   3   4

21. **Tradition:** The customary ways or the "tried and true."   1   2   3   4

22. **Obedience:** A willingness to do what God or others ask.   1   2   3   4

23. **Innovation:** Making changes that promote the ministry as it serves Christ.   1   2   3   4

24. **Initiative:** The willingness to take the first step or make the first move in a ministry situation.   1   2   3   4

25. **Other values:**

Write down all the values that you rated with a 3 or 4. Rank these according to priority. The first six are your church's actual core values.

Notes

Chapter 1 Who Is Changing?

1. Win Arn, *The Pastor's Manual for Effective Ministry* (Monrovia, CA: Church Growth, 1988), 41.

2. Aubrey Malphurs, *Advanced Strategic Planning*, 2nd ed. (Grand Rapids: Baker, 2005), 32–35.

3. Ibid., 33.

4. Tiara M. Ellis, "Christians Meet to Discuss the Scarcity of Young Ministers," *Dallas Morning News*, September 14, 2004, 5B.

5. Arn, *The Pastor's Manual*, 16.

6. Lyle E. Schaller, *Forty-four Questions for Church Planters* (Nashville: Abingdon, 1991), 20.

7. "Church Planting: A Bold New Approach to Evangelism in the 90s," *Ministry*, Summer 1991, 2.

8. George Gallup Jr., *The Unchurched American—Ten Years Later* (Princeton, NJ: Princeton Religion Research Center, 1988), 2.

9. George Barna, "Unchurched People," Barna Research Online, 2005, http://www.barna .org/ FlexPage.aspx?Page=Topic&TopicID=38, 1.

10. George Barna, "One in Three Adults Is Unchurched," Barna Research Online, March 28, 2005, http://www.barna.org/FlexPage.aspx?Page=BarnaUpdate&BarnaUpdateID=185, 1.

11. George Barna, "Generational Differences," Barna Research Online, 2004, http://www .barna.org/FlexPage.aspx?Page=Topic& TopicID=22, 1.

12. Ibid., 2005.

13. Cynthia A. Woolever, *Generations of Women in the Church* (Hartford, CT: Hartford Institute for Religion Research, Hartford Seminary), 3.

14. Barna, "Unchurched People," 1.

15. David Murrow, *Why Men Hate Going to Church* (Nashville: Thomas Nelson, 2005), 7, 10, 14.

16. Barna, "Unchurched People," 2.

17. George Barna, "A Faith Revolution Is Redefining 'Church' according to New Study," Barna Research Online, October 10, 2005, http://www.barna.org/FlexPage.aspx?Page=BarnaUpdate& BarnaUpdateID+201.

18. "U.S. Attendance at Services Is Down in Poll," *Dallas Morning News*, May 28, 1994, 43A.

19. Cathy L. Grossman and Anthony DeBarros, "Still One Nation under God," *USA Today*, December 24, 2001, 2D.

20. C. Kirk Hadaway, Penny L. Marler, and Mark Chaves, "What the Polls Don't Show: A Closer Look at U.S. Church Attendance," *American Sociological Review*, December 1993, 741–52.

21. Christine Wicke, "Church Approves Land Deal," *Dallas Morning News*, August 14, 1995, 16A.

22. Randy Frazee with Lyle E. Schaller, *The Comeback Congregation* (Nashville: Abingdon, 1995), 39.

23. "Latter Day Struggles," *U.S. News and World Report*, September 28, 1992, 73.

24. Constant H. Jacquet Jr., ed., *Yearbook of Canadian and American Churches, 1988* (Nashville: Abingdon, 1989), 262; cf. Eileen W. Lindner, ed., *Yearbook of Canadian and American Churches, 2001* (Nashville: Abingdon, 2002), 348, 352.

25. *Dallas Morning News*, February 16, 2002, 1G.

26. Jacquet, *Yearbook of Canadian and American Churches, 1988*, 262; cf. Lindner, *Yearbook of American and Canadian Churches, 2001*, 348, 352.

27. "Muslim Mosques Growing at a Rapid Pace in the U.S.," Hartford Seminary, http://fact.hartsem.edu, 1.

28. Ibid.

29. Marcy E. Mullins, "A Measure of Faith," *USA Today*, December 24, 2001, 4D.

30. Ibid.

31. Ibid.

32. Thom S. Rainer, "Shattering Myths about the Unchurched," *Southern Baptist Journal of Theology* 5, no. 1 (Spring 2001): 47.

Chapter 2 Why Are Churches Changing?

1. Carl S. Dudley and David A. Roozen, *Faith Communities Today: A Report on Religion in the United States Today* (Hartford, Conn.: Hartford Institute for Religion Research, March 2001), 10.

2. "Study: One in Four U.S. Net Users Get Religion," CNN, December 23, 2001, http://www.cnn.com.

3. George Gallup Jr. and Jim Castelli, *The People's Religion: American Faith in the 90s* (New York: Macmillan, 1989), 132–39; The Princeton Religion Research Center, *The Unchurched American . . . Ten Years Later* (Princeton: The Princeton Religion Research Center, n.d.), 2, 7.

4. Robert Bezilla, ed., *Religion in America: 1992–1993* (Princeton: Princeton Religion Research Center, 1993), 44, 57, 62; Robert Bezilla, "Religion Index Hits Ten-Year High," *Emerging Trends*, March 1996, 1–2.

5. Bezilla, *Religion in America*, 45.

6. Wade Clark Roof and William McKinney, *American Mainline Religion: Its Changing Shape and Future* (New Brunswick, NJ: Rutgers University Press, 1987), 44, 56.

7. Ibid.

8. George Barna, "A Faith Revolution Is Redefining 'Church' according to New Study," Barna Research Online, http://www.barna.org/FlexPage.aspx?Page=BarnaUpdate& Barna UpdateID+201.

9. Donald E. Messer, "Reinventing the Church," *Religion on Line*, December 12, 2001, www.religion-online.org, 1.

10. Ibid.

11. William Easum, *Dancing with Dinosaurs: Ministry in a Hostile and Hurting World* (Nashville: Abingdon, 1993), 15.

12. Ibid.

13. "The Year's Most Intriguing Findings," Barna Research Online, December 17, 2001, http://www.barna.org, 2.

14. "Worship Attendance Falls to Pre-September 11 Levels," *Dallas Morning News*, December 1, 2001, 5G.

15. Ibid.

16. George Barna, "How America's Faith Has Changed Since 9/11," Barna Research Online, November 26, 2001, http://www.barna.org, 1.

17. "Gallup Poll Topics: A–Z," The Gallup Organization, December 13, 2001, http://www.gallup.com, 1.

18. Barna, "How America's Faith Has Changed," 1.

19. Ibid., 4.

20. Rainer, "Shattering Myths about the Unchurched," 47.

21. "Worship Attendance Falls," 5G.

22. "The Year's Most Intriguing Findings," 1.

23. Rainer, "Shattering Myths about the Unchurched," 47.

24. "The Year's Most Intriguing Findings," 3.

25. Ibid.

26. Ibid., 2.

Chapter 3 Should Churches Change?

1. Charles C. Ryrie, *A Survey of Bible Doctrine* (Chicago: Moody, 1972), 38.

Chapter 4 Doing Church

1. I have written an entire book dedicated to this one topic: *Doing Church: A Biblical Guide for Leading Ministries through Change* (Grand Rapids: Kregel, 1999).

2. I cover these principles in far greater detail and depth in *Doing Church*.

3. See pages 22–25 in my book *Being Leaders* (Grand Rapids: Baker, 2003) for a more complete discussion of this concept.

Chapter 5 The Changing Church

1. J. Scott Horrell, my friend and fellow faculty member at Dallas Seminary, teaches in the theology department and has written *From the Ground Up* (Grand Rapids: Kregel, 2004) and argues for the four functions of the church: evangelism/mission, worship, learning, fellowship.

2. D. James Kennedy, *Evangelism Explosion*.

3. Steve Sjogren, *Conspiracy of Kindness* (Ventura, CA: Servant, 1993).

4. Francis Schaeffer, *The Church at the End of the Twentieth Century* (Wheaton: Crossway, 1970), 68.

Chapter 7 Defining Church

1. Malphurs, *Being Leaders*, pp. 22–25.

Chapter 9 The Thinking Church

1. Bill and Lynne Hybels, *Rediscovering Church* (Grand Rapids: Zondervan, 1995).

2. Mike Metzger, "Trick or Treat . . . or Treacherous?" *Clapham Commentary*, October 4, 2005, newsletters@claphaminstitute.org.

Chapter 10 The Strategizing Church

1. Aubrey Malphurs, *Planting Growing Churches for the 21st Century* (Grand Rapids: Baker, 2004).

2. Aubrey Malphurs and Steve Stroope, *Money Matters* (Grand Rapids: Baker, 2006).

Index

Aubrey Malphurs is the president of The Malphurs Group, a church consulting and training service, and serves as professor at Dallas Theological Seminary. He is also the author of several books on church growth and leadership, including *Value-Driven Leadership* and *Planting Growing Churches for the 21st Century*.